Library and Information Science Research
in the 21st Century

CHANDOS
INFORMATION PROFESSIONAL SERIES

Series Editor: Ruth Rikowski
(email: Rikowskigr@aol.com)

Chandos' new series of books are aimed at the busy information professional. They have been specially commissioned to provide the reader with an authoritative view of current thinking. They are designed to provide easy-to-read and (most importantly) practical coverage of topics that are of interest to librarians and other information professionals. If you would like a full listing of current and forthcoming titles, please visit our web site www.chandospublishing.com or email info@chandospublishing.com or telephone +44 (0) 1223 891358.

New authors: we are always pleased to receive ideas for new titles; if you would like to write a book for Chandos, please contact Dr Glyn Jones on email gjones@chandospublishing.com or telephone number +44 (0) 1993 848726.

Bulk orders: some organisations buy a number of copies of our books. If you are interested in doing this, we would be pleased to discuss a discount. Please email info@chandospublishing.com or telephone +44 (0) 1223 891358.

Library and Information Science Research in the 21st Century

A guide for practising librarians and students

IBIRONKE O. LAWAL

Chandos Publishing

Oxford · Cambridge · New Delhi

Chandos Publishing
TBAC Business Centre
Avenue 4
Station Lane
Witney
Oxford OX28 4BN
UK
Tel: +44 (0) 1993 848726
Email: info@chandospublishing.com
www.chandospublishing.com

Chandos Publishing is an imprint of Woodhead Publishing Limited

Woodhead Publishing Limited
Abington Hall
Granta Park
Great Abington
Cambridge CB21 6AH
UK
www.woodheadpublishing.com

First published in 2009

ISBN:
978 1 84334 372 1

British Library Cataloguing-in-Publication Data.
A catalogue record for this book is available from the British Library.

Typeset by Domex e-Data Pvt. Ltd.
Printed in the UK and USA.

Printed in the UK by 4edge Limited - www.4edge.co.uk

Contents

Acknowledgements

This book is dedicated to all library and information science students and practising librarians. My gratitude goes to Renee Bosman, John Glover and Teresa Doherty, my colleagues at Virginia Commonwealth University for reading some chapters of the manuscript and giving me valuable feedback. My sincere appreciation goes to Karen Cary, for her unflinching support. I want to thank my husband for his understanding love and devotion during the preparation of this manuscript. Finally, I thank Dr Glyn Jones for giving me this opportunity.

List of figures and tables

Figures

Tables

About the author

Ibironke Lawal holds a PhD in Education from Virginia Commonwealth University where she is currently Associate Professor and Engineering & Science Librarian. Before that, she was Physical Science Reference Librarian at Dartmouth College between 1992 and 1995 and Coordinator of Science Branch Libraries University of Virginia, Charlottesville, between 1995 and 2000. She is also an adjunct faculty at Catholic University of America, School of Library and Information Science, since 2004.

Ibironke Lawal is the author of several scholarly publications, including one that won the 2003 American Society for Engineering Education-Engineering Libraries Division Best Paper Award.

Preface

The impetus for writing this book stems from my own experience. In 2001, I was a participant in the Association of Research Library Leadership and Career Development Program that prepares middle managers for leadership roles in the upper echelons of the library and information profession. One of the requirements of the programme was to conduct a research study on any topic of interest. The idea was to guide us through the research process, from identifying a conceptual framework for a research study, selection of a topic, conductng the research, writing and publishing the report. It was then that I became aware of my lack of knowledge and expertise of the whole research process. Needless to say that my library education did not adequately prepare me for this challenge. I learned the conduct and evaluation of research during my doctoral programme in education.

An examination of the curricula of several schools of library and information science, shows that the research component exists as only one 3-credit hour course and may not be required to earn the Master's degree. A review of the literature concerning this lack of the research tradition and whether to categorize library and information profession as a science or a practice is featured in Chapter 2. My goal in writing this book, is to present a research primer, that may help prepare library practitioners and students to conduct their own research in this digital age. In addition, library professionals at all levels will derive great benefits from the book in terms of its capacity to make them competent research consumers and evaluators.

The book is set in an academic environment though the principles may apply to other situations and settings. The uniqueness of the book lies in its emphasis on the power of the digital medium and the advantages and disadvantages that it could bring to the research process. This is not a comprehensive research methods book. It is intended only as a simple guide to librarians and students. As a result, the book will not make you an expert researcher but gives adequate examples and references to relevant resources. Some areas of the book may be too elementary for some readers. This cannot be helped if the goal is to provide very basic information in the research process.

'Library and information science professionals', 'library practioners' and 'information scientists' are used throughout this book to mean mainly librarians. Though the focus slightly tilts towards academic librarianship, the main principles apply to public, school, and special libraries as well. As the title states, the emphasis is on the digital age, but the fundamentals of research remain the same in the digital as it is in the print era. Wherever possible, attention is drawn to the contrast between the two. I believe this book will help those who are interested in conducting research but until now did not know how to begin.

How is the book organized?

Chapter 1 gives the historical background of library and information science. Chapter 2 discusses the importance of research and its place in library and information science. Chapter 3 gives a brief description of the research process, Chapter 4, research designs, Chapter 5, data collection and Chapter 6 discusses data analysis for both quantitative and qualitative methods. In Chapter 7, collaboration is examined as an important element in research and scholarship and, finally, in Chapter 8, suggestions for publishing the findings in professional journals are given.

Introduction

We must never expect to find in a dogma the explanation of the system which pops it up. That explanation must be sought in its history.

John Jay Chapman

Brief history of librarianship

Most accounts of the development of the profession of librarianship in the USA suggest 1876 as the year in which the profession emerged. However, the first librarians' conference in the USA was held in 1853, which gives the impression that librarianship may have emerged before 1876. On 15 September 1853, 82 delegates, mostly from the book trade, gathered in New York City at the first library conference. The event was planned by five men: Charles Coffin Jewett (Smithsonian Institution Library Director, elected as the conference President), Charles Benjamin Norton (New York publisher), Seith Hastings Grant (New York Mercantile Library Director); Reuben Aldridge Guild (Brown University Library Director) and Daniel Coit Gilman (Johns Hopkins President) (Wiegand, 2002). According to Jewett, the goal of the conference was to provide for the diffusion of knowledge of good books for enlarging the means of public access to them. Jewett said in his speech, 'I unite most cordially in the hope which I have expressed this morning, that this convention may be the precursor of a permanent and highly useful association' (Wiegand, 2002).

Outside events, specifically the establishment of the territories of Kansas and Nebraska and the relative civil conflicts prevented another such gathering until 1876. Three events established 1876 as the year librarianship was born in the USA: (1) the first issue of the *Library Journal*, founded as *The American Library Journal*; (2) the 1876 conference in Philadelphia that led to the inception of the American Library Association (ALA); and (3) the publication of *The Public Libraries in the United States of America, their history, condition, and management* (1876), issued by the Bureau of Education. This publication includes recommendations regarding education for librarianship.

Training for the library and information profession: historical overview

The modern period in the history of education for librarianship began in the mid nineteenth century (Lynch, 2008). As early as 1829, the need for a library training school was recognized (Nasri, 1972). However, the need was not great since libraries were rare and collections small. As the nineteenth century progressed, libraries became more common and their collections increased in size. Colleges and universities began to accumulate formal collections, and people were soon needed to manage them. Plummer's outline of the history of library training states that prospective librarians typically had three options: (1) trial and error on the job training; (2) apprentice-style training by working in an established library and imitating what was observed; (3) taking some form of classes, personal instruction or formal training, often in the university library (Plummer, 1901, p. 417). The most commonly exercised option was some form of apprenticeship. Thus, the early history of library education showed a lack of uniformity and consistency.

The emphasis in *Public Libraries in the United States*, (1876) is on books and reading and the placements of such in American universities. In its introduction, the authors suggest an approach that differs from apprenticeship (p. xxiii):

> It is clear that the librarian must soon be called upon to assume a distinct position as something than mere custodian of books, and the scientific scope and value of his office be recognized and estimated in a becoming manner. To meet the demands that will be made on him he should be granted opportunities in instruction for all the departments of library science.

Similar developments were going on in Europe, and the authors refer to developments in Germany. In Germany the importance of this is beginning to be realized and the plan of making it a subject of special study in the universities finds its advocates. Dr Rullman, librarian of the University of Frieberg, had proposed that librarians should be specifically trained for the post, particularly in a university course of 3 years, after which there would be an examination that would lead to certification. His proposal was only intended primarily for professors and those likely to be appointed head of libraries and also referenced to another development in Europe. In 1834, Schrettinger, in his *Manual of Library Science*, advocated for a special school for educating librarians, evidence that proposals for systematic education for library science were made in Europe in the early nineteenth century and librarians in the USA were aware of them (Lynch, 2008).

Rullman (1874) proposed a curriculum that favoured the study of languages. He noted that most students in the library science programme in Germany would have completed courses in German, French, Latin and Greek. In addition, they would require knowledge of English, Italian and Spanish. Other proposed courses included:

- General history and collateral studies, e.g. diplomacy.
- Universal history of the more important literary production, with special knowledge of their scientific and bookseller's value.
- Knowledge of manuscripts.
- History of the art of printing.
- History of the book trade.
- Some knowledge of the fine arts, to enable the librarian to know the true value of engravings (copper, steel and wood), lithographs and photographs.
- The most interesting data concerning the well known libraries of the world: 'bibliothecography'.
- Library economy (administration of fiscal management).
- Practical exercises in cataloguing and classifying (especially the more difficult subjects, e.g. manuscripts and incunabula).
- Management of archives.

The structure and contents of Library and Information Science (LIS) education courses vary greatly between different types of LIS education providers in various European countries. The issue of unification of the LIS curriculum in European countries will be addressed later in this chapter.

The issue of library education continued to get attention in the USA. Those who managed university and government libraries had the necessary knowledge of the many aspects of librarianship necessary to manage those collections well. However, as the public library movement grew, fewer people had the knowledge to manage those collections well. This directed leaders in the profession to consider the issue of training and education for those who staff those libraries.

The quality of instruction in library schools was under scrutiny for several decades. This is because the contribution of Melvyl Dewey to the development of library education in the USA was blamed for the inadequacies or omissions seen in library education. He was faulted for setting the wrong direction for education in librarianship. He did not require college graduation as a prerequisite for entrance into the programme; he concentrated too heavily on technical matters, thus functioning as an extension of the apprenticeship programme, and he created an educational programme that was not research-oriented (Lynch, 2008). The Carnegie Foundation intervened as it had instituted some public libraries, and was interested in the training that the librarians would receive. The Foundation charged Alvin Saunders Johnson to examine library schools and the adequacy of their curricula. Most of Johnson's recommendations were rejected and the Carnegie Corporation invited C. C. Williamson to assess library education and make recommendations for its future (Lynch, 2008). The Carnegie Corporation was created by Andrew Carnegie in 1911 to promote the advancement and diffusion of knowledge and understanding. One of its two major concerns was advancing education and knowledge.

In 1923, Williamson issued the first benchmark report on training competencies for the Carnegie Corporation (Williamson, 1923). He was interested in raising the quality of instruction in library science and in ensuring that it held as comfortable a place in the university hierarchy of curricula. What he found was a debate that still continues—the discrepancy between the clerical nature of positions and the education requirements. He saw no agreement between his vision of library school curricula and the clerical nature of demand for entry-level positions by library administrators. Williamson attempted to identify what kinds of training should be required for each type of work and where that training should take place (Lynch, 2008). Librarians of Williamson's time were confronted with how to organize the work of the library into different jobs and then to separate those jobs that are primarily clerical in nature from those categorized as professional.

Williamson proposed that a librarian would need a broad professional training, represented by 4 years of college and at least 1 year of graduate study in an accredited library school. Clerical work could be done by high school graduates who receive a short training in library methods that could be provided by the libraries themselves. For years, ALA Policy 54.1 acknowledges that to meet the goals of library service, both professional and supportive staff are needed in libraries (ALA, 2005), a division that still exists today. In its publication, *Library and Information Studies and Human Resources Utilization* (ALA, 2002), the ALA attempts to identify the various categories of library personnel and the levels of training and education appropriate to the personnel in the numerous categories of jobs in the library. In that document, the title 'Librarian' carries the connotation of 'professional' in the sense that professional tasks are those that require a special background and education. The title 'Librarian' therefore should be used only to designate positions in libraries that require the qualification and impose the responsibilities suggested in the document. The document recommends three categories of supportive staff listed below, followed by basic requirements:

1. *Associate specialist*—Bachelors degree (with preferred coursework in library and/or information science); *or* bachelors degree, plus additional applicable academic work.

2. *Assistant specialist*—at least 2 years of college level study, or AA degree (with or without library technical assistant training) preferred; *or* post-secondary school training and relevant skills; *or* certificate programme.

3. *Clerk*—high school diploma or equivalent.

Since Williamson's report, there had been an expansion of library jobs and specializations apart from the professional librarian's job. However, no two libraries will need the same categories of staff. Williamson alluded to this fact in his report. Each library will have to determine the jobs needed and the nature of training required to do those jobs. There are, however, no prescribed courses required for supportive staff. According to Lynch (2008), as the profession undergoes rapid change, there is a lag in making changes in job definitions. Policy 54.2 recommends the appropriate degree for librarians is the Master's degree from a programme accredited by the ALA (or from a Master's level programme in library and information studies accredited or recognized by the appropriate national body of another country) (ALA, 2005). This recommendation, with the addition of the degree obtained in another country, grew out of the Williamson report.

The curriculum is another facet of library education that has generated many controversies. Forty-seven years after Williamson, Conant (1980) attempted to address this issue. According to him, what sets a profession apart is its readiness to guarantee the competence and motivation of its members to perform in the interest of those who benefit from its service

(Conant, 1980). He went on to say that the quality of an educational programme is the responsibility of the educators, but the profession as a whole has a responsibility to work with educators in setting standards and in providing guidelines for the content and intellectual level of the training programmes (Conant, 1980). He also contended that a stronger programme attracts stronger students. Practitioners representing academic, public, school and special libraries all tended to agree that there was much wrong with library education; educators engaged in self-examination and self-criticism. The consensus that change was necessary hid the fact that there was little agreement on what these changes should be (White and Paris, 1985). One of the recommendations of White and Paris was that there should be more post-MLS continuing education, an idea supported by practitioners, educators, professional societies and government agencies who believed continuing education to be useful.

However, there was neither incentive in the form of either financial or promotional rewards for the completion of continuing education units or degrees nor was there insistence that continuing education be undertaken to safeguard regular jobs. The only incentive came from the Medical Library Association, which developed a continuing education programme that carries with it, to this day, the threat of decertification for those who do not participate. Generally, continuing education for librarians remains optional, selected by an individual primarily because of a desire to learn. Given this narrow approach to continuing education, it is highly doubtful that continuing activities will affect a significant portion of the library profession. It is likely that continuing education will continue to be an important part of the strategy for imparting new knowledge, and it may expand to some degree. It is extremely doubtful that it will provide a significant alternative to and extension of the one-time educational experience of the Master's programme. It is still probably true that for many librarians, perhaps the majority, that education received while earning the Master's degree may be their only significant professional education. This is a sad thought to contemplate in a professional environment.

The 1-year Master's programme

Most of the graduate-level library schools in Conant's study offered a curriculum that could be completed in two or three semesters with no introductory work at the undergraduate level. The range of topics covered in the 1-year programmes is given below, but none of the schools offered all of these courses.

- foundations
- library administration
- types of libraries
- technical services
- reference and bibliography
- client group services
- practicum.

The library schools concentrated on the basic functions of the profession: reference, bibliography, technical services, and administration. Beyond these subject areas, the schools offered selected concentrations in types of libraries, information science and research methods (Conant, 1980).

An international survey of competencies conducted in 2000/2001 by Rehman *et al.* concluded that a consensus was emerging on the important competencies that should be in the library and information studies curriculum (Rehman *et al.*, 2002). These competencies represent the judgements of a group of academics from North America, South-east Asia and the Arabian Gulf region as well as practitioners from the Arabian Gulf region. The most important competencies that needed to be covered in the curriculum included: knowledge of information theory, information use and users, the social context of information, information needs, ethics, information resource development concepts and processes, information organization and processing, information searching and retrieval, access services, automation and networking, Web design and searching, research capabilities, planning and evaluation, human resource skills and communication.

Graduates of the 1-year programmes did both clerical and professional tasks, because library administrators did not clearly differentiate these two jobs. According to Williamson, a shortage of people suitable for the higher grade of library service had occurred for some time and it would no doubt continue to be felt until some differentiation was recognized by library administrators in the organization of library staff between duties of clerical and routine character and those requiring professional outlook and attainments (Williamson, 1923, p. 4). Williamson also found that schools of library science in 1923 were not in the mainstream of their respective institutions. He remarked that:

> Every existing university library school is a negligible part of the institution, often unnoticed or looked down upon by the other faculties and especially by departments in which research is emphasized. The causes for this lack of prestige seem to be the smallness of the library school, the brevity of the course, the predominance of women in both faculty and student body, the preponderance of teachers having only the rank of instructors, and the total lack of anything recognized as productive-scholarship. All of these conditions are remedial and will tend to disappear as

> the standards of the library profession are gradually raised, increasing the size and importance of the professional schools.
>
> Williamson (1923, p. 71)

Library education: the case for research capabilities

The founding of the Graduate Library School (GLS) at the University of Chicago in 1926 pushed the debate of vocational versus professional emphasis in the direction of professional theory. Scholars from a variety of academic disciplines were involved from its inception. The school brought academic study and scientific research to the profession, as well as colloquia and scholarly publication. This was a benchmark for two reasons. First, the faculty was predominantly composed of members who were not librarians but mostly social scientists. Second, was the hiring of faculty with a strong research interest and, with one exception, no library experience.

The opening of a school such as Chicago's GLS would seem to fulfil the majority of Williamson's recommendations. It was instrumental in emphasizing the relationship between teaching and research and theory and practice. It undertook research, prepared textbooks and established a journal to disseminate research findings (Saiful, nd).

Although the school gained an excellent reputation, it also generated much controversy. Houser and Schrader (1978) argue that the GLS quickly lost its original intent and that the research focus of the school was watered down. The seminal issue of the scholar versus the experienced librarian continues even today. The founding of the GLS at the University of Chicago was a grand experiment that ultimately failed due to the reluctance of librarianship to accept a research-oriented school (Hurt, 1992). Carl Miliam, the president of the ALA, when planning for the GLS was initiated, voiced his concern about the direction and focus of the GLS (Richardson, 1982).

The integration of a whole new discipline of information science into the field of library science began in the 1960s. Current names of library degrees are evidence of this change; examples are Masters in the Resource Information Management (M.I.R.M.), Masters in Information Science (M.I.S.), Masters in Library and Information Science (M.L.I.S.), Masters in Library Science (M.L.S.), to mention a few (Wilson and Hermanson, 1998). With all these changes, a core curriculum was seen as essential for library education.

That concern about the focus of library science programmes continues unabated and unresolved. On one hand, librarianship wants graduates ready to move into positions without the need for further education or training; on the other hand, librarianship sees a positive value in having library science programmes exist in the milieu of higher education. Indeed, librarians seem convinced of the necessity of holding the Master's degree but seem less committed to the process of education usually required for attaining the degree (Hurt, 1992). The University of Chicago experience can be interpreted in a number of ways. One interpretation is that librarianship was not ready for scholarship (Hurt, 1992). The placement of any unit in an academic setting is not a right, but a privilege.

Basically, there are two types of institutions of higher education, research-oriented and instruction-oriented. The research-oriented institution is interested primarily in the synthesis, production, and dissemination of information and knowledge. Instruction does not necessarily become second-rate in such an institution; indeed there are those who suggest that it is enhanced by the research thrust. The instruction-oriented institution has more of the following characteristics: a greater emphasis on the quality of instruction in the institution, a greater emphasis on the undergraduate component of the institution, and a justifiable pride in the ability of its graduates to move to research-oriented institutions as graduate students.

These are two models each with different assumptions and expectations. Library science programmes exist in both types of institutions. Being a part of an institution means that the unit accepts the goals and mission of the parent institution and adjusts its own accordingly. This appears to be difficult for library science (Hurt, 1992). In the research-oriented institutions, library science is normally seen as a weak link, contributing little to the overall mission of the institution. This stems from at least two sources. First, the library science programme is normally more attentive to the instructional components than to the research components. Library science has a tradition of heavily investing its intellectual resources in instruction. This is out of step because of lack of the tradition of research that other units in the institution garnered.

The second reason library science is often considered a weak link in the research-oriented institution is its professional school focus. Professional schools are ill-understood within research-oriented institutions. The strength of most research-oriented institutions does not lie in their professional schools and where there are strong professional programmes; the clear emphasis is on both academic quality and quality research.

Within instruction-based institutions, library science is sometimes considered an anomaly. One reason is that there is no undergraduate programme leading to the master's degree programmes. In an institution that places its emphasis on undergraduate instruction, programmes such as library science appear to be incomplete.

Two models exist for library science programmes in academic institutions. The first is the professional school approach and the second is the academic programme approach. The apprentice mode of learning was a comfortable concept for librarianship. This evolved into a mind-set of professional education, especially in the years following Williamson (1923). Virtually every professional programme in higher education has made its programme more academically based, with the exception of library science. The academic model assumes that library science is an academic unit and will operate under the same rules and as other academic units.

Although education's aim is twofold—the pursuit and attainment of knowledge and the preparation for productive careers—library science focuses mostly on the second. Robbins-Carter and Seavey (1986) report that employers seem to prefer graduates from a programme accredited by the ALA but are not interested in specific coursework, except in school media. Further, there is evidence that additional or specialized degrees are not rewarded by the profession in higher salary scales (White and Paris, 1985). The provision of librarians that have skills to start work on the first day, as opposed to education for a lifelong profession is the root of the dialectic.

In the July 2005 ALA draft of core competencies, a statement under the heading 'Knowledge inquiry: research' reads:

> Understands the nature of research, research, methods and research findings within the library and information fields and has an awareness of current literature in these and related areas. The librarian is familiar with the fundamentals of research survey and data collection designs of current or potential value to library and information settings.

Standard I of the ALA standards for Accreditation of Master's Programmes in Library and Information Studies, adopted in 1993 states:

> the essential character of the field of library and information studies; that is, recordable information and knowledge, and the services and technologies to facilitate their management and use, encompassing information and knowledge creation, communication, identification, selection, acquisition, organization and description, storage and retrieval, preservation, analysis, interpretation, evaluation, synthesis, dissemination, and management.
>
> The importance of research to the advancement of the field's knowledge base.
>
> ALA (2008)

Both of these quotations from the ALA signify that they recognize the importance of research knowledge in library education.

In the UK, the curriculum for library and information science courses at both undergraduate and postgraduate level is based on the needs of the modern information professionals (Saiful, nd). The compulsory modules at the Masters level include:

- Information characteristics/use/requirements
- Information policy
- Information sources, organization and retrieval
- Development of information products and services
- Optional modules from:
  - Knowledge management
  - Database management systems
- Digital libraries.

In the USA a compulsory module for the MLIS programme includes:

- Information society
- Organization of information
- Information sources and services
- Research methods and statistics
- Information systems and technology
- Management and marketing information.

Conant (1980) studied the contributions of library education to the future of the profession. He interviewed faculty in 14 accredited library schools and one non-accredited library school that offered the Master's degree. The responses were a mixture of praise and condemnation, of optimism and pessimism, of justification for shortcomings and realistic appraisal of the educators' limitations. The principal finding of this portion of the inquiry is the gap of understanding and communication between educators and practitioners. This gap is hard to assess but the evidence of it is strong from interviews with both the educators and the practitioners.

There is an insufficient integration of theoretical research and the conceptual analysis of practical problems in librarianship, due to the inability of practitioners (limited by scarce resources) to apply the findings of theoretical research. Lester (1990) called this the 'identity issue'. He acknowledges that the identity issue is two-pronged: what practising librarians identify as the role of education for librarianship; and library education's identity as embodied by the library school's relationship with the university (Lester, 1990).

Historically, there has been a tension between practitioners and library school faculty over what should constitute education for librarianship. In 1994, the conflict seemed to have escalated. Practitioners, feeling pressured by both changing technologies and the increasingly sophisticated information needs of their patrons, appeared persuaded that education for librarianship must provide entrants to the field with specific preparation for their areas of specialization in order to function effectively in their jobs. The practising librarian's litany of complaints was long and diverse. They criticized the library schools for not providing potential academic research librarians with a specific set of competencies, and for not instructing new professionals on how to be 100% productive on their first day on the job (Lester, 1990). In 1997, a quartet of library schools overhauled their curricula to meet the needs of the twenty-first century. These are: University of Michigan, Drexel University, University of Illinois, Urbana-Champaign and Florida State University. The role of the librarian in the twenty-first century will bear little resemblance to that of the typical librarian of the past (Marcum, 1997).

As seen by the working professional, the gap between educators and practitioners results from an alleged scarcity of research by library school faculty that might contribute to the improvement of libraries and librarianship. Furthermore, according to interviews, the educators have estranged themselves from the working professionals by failing to encourage a flow of personnel from libraries to library school faculty and back. Some working librarians say that library school faculty positions have been staffed in recent years by doctoral graduates who have had little or no library experience. Furthermore, it is said few working librarians are invited to join library school faculty because of concerns of university and library school administrators that the standing of the school and the quality of instruction might suffer.

These allegations could be countered by contrary evidence in certain graduate schools. Faculty members and doctoral students are doing research on contemporary library problems at Rutgers, Case-Western Reserve, Chicago, Berkeley, Michigan, Illinois, Florida, UCLA and Columbia, all of which have doctoral programmes. All of the schools in the Conant study have faculty members who have had recent library and field experience. Additionally, doctoral candidates are typically required to have had experience prior to entering the programme.

The single most critical issue facing library science education has to do with the tensions between professional and academic expectations (Auld, 1990). Practitioners expect library school graduates to be prepared to undertake a significant commitment to being a professional in the library community, while academics expect library school graduates to be budding researchers who should eschew professional commitment. These conflicting expectations have a relatively small area of intersection.

The academic model at its most extreme form places primary emphasis on research (demonstrated through prolific publication), permits a secondary emphasis on teaching (but the good researcher should have sufficient grants on hand to avoid this demeaning task) and only grudgingly concedes a possible tertiary activity (certainly not an emphasis) on service. It is argued that it is only by doing research can an instructor bring intellectual excitement and currency to the classroom.

Why library schools fail

A problem with library education is evident in several school closures, many between 1978 and 1990. A study of four of these closures showed that the school administrations and faculty were isolated from their local academic peers. Those library educators who had served on university committees were often perceived as out of touch and out of date by other faculty. One vice president recalled, the library school had become isolated ... and was not participating, people didn't know them in a social way. They knew them in a scholarly way, but as being out of date. But there was something more here than tiredness; there was dead wood in the sense of not being interested in the way the world was changing.

Paris (1988, p. 90).

It is possible that some of the library educators had failed to reach out from some reluctance (or inability) to 'explain library and information science,' as several of the faculty informants claimed was necessary when they met with outsiders. Another vice president charged that

there was hardly a single faculty member who was known to any other faculty member [of the university] ... No one had met anyone from [the business school], the department of computer science, or the department of management information systems. They didn't know where the computer labs were on campus. Insularity proved to be a disaster.

Paris (1988, p. 109)

Insufficient or inappropriate faculty research was cited in two of the cases, an external evaluation noted that research was 'not visible in current and impressive depth' and that 'significant' productivity was necessary (Paris, 1988, p. 88). At that same university, after a task force had begun exploring the possibility of a reorganized information management programme, a member of the panel warned that if the university was going to have a library science programme, it should be at the cutting edge of current research (Paris, 1988, p. 99). While this could be a welcome statement for one faculty member, another moaned that the administration wanted them to become another MIT (Paris, p. 84).

Library education programmes that evolved from the past shared at least four attributes: (1) strong, imaginative, forward-looking leadership; (2) sound teaching that might inspire the next generation to be better; (3) a timely and relevant research agenda; and (4) a strong mission. All highly rated schools had doctoral programmes, and it could be argued that this was essential for attracting the research-oriented faculty that gave the institution high prestige (White, 1983, p. 257).

The issue of disconnect in library education is still being discussed today, as evidenced by Michael Gorman's forums in library education at some ALA conferences (Annual 2005 and 2006) bear testimony to this. With the proliferation of online courses, and fewer face-to-face class time library education is still a concern for some library educators and directors.

European perspective

European countries aim towards an internationalization of Library and Information Studies. Bologna Process is currently the major reform of Higher Education in Europe. It aims at creating a Higher Education Area by 2010, in which students can choose from a wide range of high-quality courses and benefit from transparent procedures. Forty countries are now involved in the Bologna process. The goal is to facilitate student mobility and improve employability in Europe. The focus is on the recognition of qualifications. In central and southern Europe, LIS departments coexist with other forms of on-the-job training offered by national libraries, other libraries and cultural institutions (Harbo, 1996). A new structure and curriculum for LIS education is now being proposed in the document *European Curriculum Reflections on Library and Information Science Education* (2005).

Conclusions

Librarianship started as a vocation, not a profession. Hence, library education and training was originally provided in the form of apprenticeship and vocational training. Melvyl Dewey's proposal for library education was seen to be inadequate in moving librarianship forward as a profession. Williamson on the other hand was the first to propose that librarians would need a broad training for at least 1 year after obtaining the bachelor's degree. Conant examined the objectives, scope and content of library education in a few representative accredited library schools. At that time, the profession was faced with a shortage of librarians. His conclusion was that the library profession needed to develop a coherent basis for its claim to professionalism. He believed that to achieve this, non-professional training has to be separated from professional training and the quality and content of the master's programme, needed to be improved. The debate of the library school curriculum is still going on today.

2

The significance of research in the library and information profession

Both the study of library science and the practice of librarianship in the USA are relatively young fields of endeavour. Librarianship as we know it today originated in 1876 when the American Library Association (ALA) was founded as the first national organization designed to promote the interests and activities of librarians and libraries. The first library school affiliated with an institution of higher education was founded in 1887 at Columbia University as the School of Library Economy. In a history of the school, Ray Tautman wrote:

> The old school of Library Economy began almost by accident, though nurtured by and developed according to the ideas of its zealous founder [Melvil Dewey]. The Trustees of the College, who had grudgingly permitted its establishment happily abolished the school within a few years.
>
> Tautman (1954, p. vii)

For several decades after the first library school had been established within an academic setting, education for librarianship (or 'training' as it was called) was conducted on the job, in library classes in library schools, or by means of apprenticeships sponsored by libraries. Because most of this early training developed directly from library practices, education for librarianship was initially closely tied to both basic tasks and routines performed by librarians (Martin, 1957). The strong emphasis on library work experience and practice has dominated library education for many decades; and is still discernible today (Busha, 1981).

The library and information science (LIS) profession has been debating the library school curriculum for over five decades. The problem with the curriculum lies in the idea that librarianship is said to possess a service ideal but not a body of theoretical knowledge (Shaughnessy, 1976). This sets it apart from other professions such as teaching and psychology. Theoretical knowledge is generally developed through a process of research, as opposed to knowledge based on practice. LIS has not had a long tradition of the research. Those who have assessed the body of research of librarians have agreed that both the quantity and quality are somewhat inadequate (Powell and Connaway, 2004). For example, Ennis (1967) described library research as 'noncummulative, fragmentary, generally weak and relentlessly oriented to immediate practice' (Grotzinger, 1981). While collection and publication of library statistics is not research, it is less clear whether or not to consider, an account of the history of a library, the results of a questionnaire study, or a detailed survey of a given library as research (Goldhor, 1972, p. 1).

Scanning the curricula of some LIS programmes the dearth of research courses is clearly noticeable. In some library schools, research methods course is not required, leaving the students to make the choice of whether or not to develop a research-oriented culture. This has far reaching implications for graduates of the Master's programme, the programme's place in the research university, and for the relation of the profession to other professions. As research is not essential to library training, many professional librarians do not possess the necessary expertise to do their own research for the purposes of promotion, professional advancement or interest.

What is research?

Research is a term loosely used to describe a variety of activities such as collecting masses of information, examining esoteric theories, and producing innovative new products. It is important for a student or practitioner embarking on a programme of research to have a clear idea of what the word 'research' means (Walliman, 2005). Walliman identified four ways the word is being erroneously used:

> First, simply as a mere gathering of facts or information a student who has been told to prepare a presentation on a subject completely unknown to him might say, 'I will go and do a little bit of research on the subject'. He may read some books and magazines, and possibly check some Internet sites to become better informed about the subject. Second, the term is used to describe moving facts from one situation to another. For example, a practitioner who needs to come up with justification for a large purchase might look at evidence of use of library materials and interlibrary loan records, which will show how many times an item was borrowed from another library. On the basis of this, assemble a report that can inform decision. As with collection of facts, this is an important component of research but not its entirety. Third, research is thought of as a peculiar activity far removed from practical life,

though, it is often forgotten that the activity of research has greatly influenced all aspects of our daily lives and has shaped our understanding of the world around us. Fourth, it is used as a word to attract notices, people use the word to make an impression, to draw attention to a product, making a statement like 'years of research have gone into making of this product'.

Walliman (2005, p. 8)

One of the characteristics of human beings is the desire to better understand their existence and the world about them. This want can be partially fulfilled by knowledge gained from everyday occurrences or by the formulation of generalizations based on first-hand experience. However, a more efficient and effective approach to expanding knowledge is the conduct of specially planned and structured investigation—a process known as 'research' (Busha and Harter, 1980). This chapter discusses the definition of research, specifically LIS research. It also discusses the significance and importance of LIS research in the digital age.

There is no one definition of research, 'in part because there is more than one kind of research' (Powell and Connaway, 2004, p. 1). Research may be defined as the systematic attempt to discover new facts or new relationships among facts by means of the formulation of a preliminary explanation, or hypotheses, which is subjected to an appropriate, objective investigation for verification or disproof in terms that can be expressed in a general way (Shera, 1964). Hernon (1991) offers a more precise definition focused on the types of research in LIS. He defines research as 'an inquiry process that has clearly defined parameters and has as its aim, the: discovery or creation of knowledge, or theory building; testing, confirmation, revision, refutation of knowledge and theory; and/or investigation of a problem for local decision making' (Hernon, 1991, p. 3).

Busha and Harter (1980) describe research as a 'systematic quest for knowledge'. Morris (2002, p. 1), calls it an ill-defined word. He contends that there is little agreement about what it embraces and what it is for. Broadly speaking, research can be defined as any conscious premeditated inquiry—any investigation that seeks to increase one's knowledge of a given situation. By this definition both the compilation of statistics and the high school student's term paper are research. A more explicit definition is that by Goldhor (1972, p. 3): 'Research is one which uses the scientific method of inquiry and uses it in order to establish or disestablish the truth or a given relationship, in short, to test a hypothesis.' In this book, research is used to mean the process of conducting a study with accompanying statistical analysis to interpret the results and draw conclusions or formulate theories.

With its origin in science, research begins with a question: Why or How? It is a process of creating new knowledge among a community of learners that includes undergraduates, graduate students, faculty and community members. In the scientific community, research is undertaken to address problems of significance or to increase or fill gaps in bodies of theoretical knowledge. The increasing desire to expand knowledge in the library and information field is necessary because of globalization and the fast advancing technological age. Undoubtedly, many other ways exist by which a problem can be explored and knowledge accumulated, such as intuition, serendipity, or the discovery of truth by accident, but none can compete with authentic, empirical research.

Librarianship today is particularly in need of the generalized truths that scientific research is designed to uncover. Librarians may have had extensive practical experience, much of which has been recorded; there may have been reasonably large accumulations of raw data; and the literature may have records of many perceptive persons thinking about the problems. But until this can be stated into universal generalizations or laws based on evidence and confirmable by further observations, librarianship will remain an art or field of practice and will not become a science or discipline (Goldhor, 1972, p. 2). Most contributions to the study of libraries have focused more on gathering data that allow library phenomena to be identified and described, but do not follow through with statistical analyses that can explain why and how? Busha and Harter (1980) believe many investigators' distrust of theory has contributed to a neglect of basic research in the field. One reason for this situation may be the inadequate attention that library schools have given to research methods instruction. Instead, many scholars in librarianship have tended to rely upon basic knowledge gleaned from other disciplines such as sociology, education and psychology. Thus, the LIS field would be receptive to the conduct of numerous kinds of basic inquiry.

If librarianship is to become a science, the first requirement is that there be people able to do research; the second requirement is that there be also people who are able to assess the research produced—to reject the bad and accept the good, and to make further improvements in the results as their power and experience enable them (Goldhor, 1972). As in the past, librarianship is currently almost exclusively dependent on knowledge that is acquired by trial and error experience and not yet systematized into scientific laws and theories. Individual librarians gather data or make objective observations of operating effectiveness, and take note of advantages, limitations and other features of each task. This is far from the development of a theory that will satisfactorily account for the behaviour of people in regard to library's collections and services. Only the method of scientific research could take the profession in the direction it needs to be today. Goldhor (1972) thought theories developed through such scientific research might well provide, or at best lend support to the long sought philosophy of librarianship.

Many of the concerns voiced about library science since 1960 have been directed toward the inabilities of some graduate library schools to help improve the status and quality of inquiry and scholarship. For example, Jackson (1963) underscored the lack of co-ordination among library schools in both the conduct of research and in the teaching of methodologies for inquiry. Also, Wynar (1970) expressed the need for the incorporation of statistical methods into the curricula of library schools. He pointed out that librarians need knowledge of the process of statistical analysis of quantified data, citing the following trends as bases for the need: (1) the social sciences, of which librarianship is a part, are increasingly dependent upon the quantification of data to obtain solid evidence for decision making, and (2) librarians are being called upon to accomplish more data analyses as library operations are increasingly subjected to careful scrutiny. Wynar also contends that sound research depends upon sound research practices, and as the application of statistics often enters into research problems at various points, the outcome of the entire research project depends upon the understanding of the statistical method. The situation may be different now than when Wynar wrote his book over three decades ago, but the changes still have not kept pace with changes in other disciplines.

Incorporation of statistical analysis into the curricula comes under the umbrella of research method instruction. Research methods in the plural, is generally taken to mean all the specific techniques used to secure, record, measure or analyse raw data. Usually, these are summed up into a few main groups of methods, for example, the historical method of research, the survey method or the statistical method, which all relate to technical procedures that are selected because of the nature of the data in question. In the singular, the term research method means either the whole process or cycle of research, from the identification of a problem to the writing of the final report, or the general framework of concepts, assumptions and procedures that constitute the scientific method of inquiry. The second meaning is the one used in this book.

Origin of the research enterprise in library and information science

In 1926, the Graduate Library School at the University of Chicago was established as a result of a million-dollar grant from the Carnegie Corporation. In 1931, *The Library Quarterly* was founded at the University of Chicago, the first scholarly journal in the field of American librarianship to be devoted primarily to the publication of reports of completed research. The lead article in the initial issue of the publication was entitled 'The place of research in Library Science'. It was a reprint of an address delivered by Charles C. Williamson in 1930 at Case Western Reserve University. Williamson stated that if the library is to rise to its responsibility as a social institution and educational force, it must attack problems by the application of methods of research that are being found effective in every other field (Williamson, 1931).

Justification for research methods course in the library and information science core curriculum

Today, the need for research in library science has become even more critical because the world has witnessed a technological and scientific revolution since Williamson's speech. These technological advances coupled with the exponential growth of information, the changes in political, economic and social realms, and increased globalization have profoundly affected the habits of millions of people. In addition, the world population is more literate, sophisticated, demanding, and has higher expectations of library service. People move around the globe and the world is becoming flat. Libraries are expected to provide services to a more diverse population now than ever. These phenomena have altered almost all human communication patterns.

Beginning in the 1970s, the first online bulletin board system (BBS) let people with both computers and access to telephone lines swap documents, read news online and send one another messages. Usenet groups of communities with similar interests became popular in the 1980s (Palfrey and Gasser, 2008).

The advent of the Internet in the early 1990s and subsequently the World Wide, Web and search engines completely revolutionized the information industry. In 2001, Polaroid declared bankruptcy because of the prevalence of digital cameras and in 2006, Tower Records, liquidated its stores after 46 years in the music industry largely because of the popularity of online music sharing and retail. One of the earliest online music sharing outfits was Napster, which later became an online music retailer. By 2008, i-Tunes had become the largest music retailer in the USA. Today, most young people carry mobile devices such as cell phones, iPhones, PDAs and iPods. These are some of the most rapid technological transformation of all times. For example, on 6 March 2007, ComScore Networks, a leader in measuring the digital communication announced that 747 million people age 15 and over used the Internet worldwide in January 2007, a 10% increase over that of January 2006.

The fast moving technological revolution has had the most dramatic impact on the younger population. The expectations and behaviours of this group will have a significant impact on the nature of the services that public and academic libraries need to plan and provide (Abram and Luther, 2004). The vocabulary of information has exploded as we transitioned into the twenty-first century. Three decades ago, words such as Wikis, Blogs, Podcasting, RSS feeds, 'Second life', Myspace and Facebook were not in use. New tools or devices seem to enter our lives everyday.

Digital Natives versus Digital Immigrants

The young generation of the twenty-first century are said to be 'born with a chip' (Abram and Luther, 2004). Born in the digital age and having grown up with technology, their world is full of computers, cell phones, i-pods, cable television and instant messengers. According to Pensky (2001), today's average college graduates have spent less than 5000 hours of their lives reading, but over 10,000 hours playing video games and 20,000 hours watching television. Pensky calls this demographic known to be native speakers of the digital language, Digital Natives or the cyber generation. In order for schools to adapt to the habits of Digital Natives and how they are processing information, educators need to accept that the mode of learning is changing rapidly in a digital age. What they expect to do in college and what faculty members and institutions of higher education are providing could result in a problematic mismatch of sizable proportion (Palfrey and Gasser, 2008). Digital Natives expect instant responses to requests, they multitask and are more likely to figure things out on their own than to ask for help. To them, research is more likely a Google search than a trip to the library. They are more likely to check in with the Wikipedia community, or to turn to another online friend, than they are to ask a reference librarian for help. They rarely, if ever, buy the newspaper in hard copy; instead, they graze through copious amounts of news and other information online (Palfrey and Gasser, 2008). They have influence on their parents, grandparents, siblings and other older members of the population who all have to learn this digital language in order to interact meaningfully with them. (This group could be called Digital Immigrants, that is, the 'analog generation'.)

No major aspect of modern life is untouched by information technologies. Business can be done more quickly and over greater distances, often starting with a small amount of money. Most notable are the way digital technologies have transformed peoples' lives and the way they connect to others. Politicians, religious leaders, teachers, community leaders and sporting industries have all been transformed by the new technologies in the way they communicate with their constituents. Digital Natives are constantly connected with friends and associates in real space and in virtual worlds. They rely on this virtual space for all the information they need. They chat on Instant Messenger (IM) instead of writing letters; they visit with loved ones using web cams and they text messages on their phones instead of writing e-mails, they use Skype instead of face to face meetings. The Digital Natives are inspired by globalization.

With all that is going on in this digital age, the LIS curriculum needs a transformation and some leaders of the profession are aware of this fact. According to Gorman (2003a), LIS schools are reporting that their students are demographically different from the library school students of 20 years ago. He also states that there are fewer traditional students and more non-traditional students who are changing careers in mid-life due to the unavailability of jobs in academia, changes in personal lives, or other reasons. All these call for either a revamping or abolition of the current curriculum in favour of an entirely new one (Gorman, 2003b). Gorman believes that in twenty-first century America, LIS schools should turn out graduates well grounded in the traditional subjects of cataloguing, reference, acquisitions and collection development, library instruction, specialized fields of librarianship such as school librarianship, public librarianship as well as courses that are appropriate for the digital age (web development, electronic communication, etc.). The traditional courses form the core of the professional education and should not be minimized but revised to meet today's information needs. Though a research methods course is not on Gorman's list, its inclusion as a core course in all LIS schools curriculum could be instrumental to growing theoretical knowledge for the profession.

Another reason for revamping the LIS curriculum is the emergence of electronic communication that has become the norm rather than the exception. Because Digital Natives are more comfortable with digital media more library services are now being delivered electronically. Over 20 years ago, Swisher and McClure said that LIS professionals were faced with a broad range of challenges and opportunities to improve the effectiveness of their organizations, to respond better to the information needs of their communities, and to provide leadership in the information environment, a statement as true today as it was then (Swisher and McClure, 1984). Budget size, staff and the number of people using the library's resources all remain critical pieces for library assessment. Those who fund libraries want to hold libraries accountable for failures in delivering services.

As the role and perception of libraries continue to change in the twenty-first century, the way we evaluate libraries is also changing. The path to both successful library services and increased organizational effectiveness calls for skills and competencies beyond daily operational skills. The prerequisite skills to address such challenges and opportunities are in areas of producing and understanding research (Swisher and McClure, 1984). Conducting research and presenting the results in a most convincing way have become more important now than ever. Research allows one to gain an appreciation for the practical applications of knowledge and to learn about theories, tools, resources and ethical issues that scholars and professionals encounter on a daily basis. One will learn how to formulate questions, design plans to find answers, collect and analyse data, draw conclusions from that data and share findings with a community. Learning about research will also make one more informed consumer of research. One will be able to better evaluate the information presented and make informed decision about public policy issues that affect one's everyday life. Research prepares one for the world beyond tenure by honing one's independent thinking and creativity, time management and budget management skills, and confidence in one's academic and career goals.

Most professions or disciplines have established a body of knowledge emanating from years of research, which forms the basis upon which the profession operates. Although LIS has been called an occupation grounded in techniques and personal arts rather than a discipline or profession, there is still a body of research, and new additions continually appear (Hernon, 1991). All of this research may add knowledge and make a contribution to the profession, but not all are significant enough to get cited. Pendlebury (1991) stated that the number of uncited social science articles written in 1984 was 74.7%. However, without the *marginalia* (reviews, notes, meeting abstracts, editorials, obituaries, letters), the number shrinks to 48.0%, which is still a high number. The marginalia forms only 27% of the items indexed by the Institute for Scientific Information (ISI) in the *Social Science Citation Index* for 1984. However, whether or not research is cited should not be a deterrent to conducting future research. The need still exists for research that not only offers an examination of phenomena in the field but also forges a relationship with other disciplines, both to learn from other fields and also to communicate to them the value of LIS and the importance of the questions addressed (Hernon, 1999).

Librarianship in the USA has traditionally been a problem-oriented field; librarians have tended to focus more attention on practical problems in the 'real world' than they have on theoretical issues. Yet, communication patterns of the past can no longer be assumed to be adequate in today's environment. The conduct of research will help with learning the best ways to interact with the world's new generation of information consumers both within and outside the LIS profession.

The search for new library science knowledge has historically been assigned a rather low priority; it appears that librarians in the early decades of the twentieth century were preoccupied with more pressing and immediate demands. For example, purchasing, processing and organizing library materials were foremost in their agenda. Systematic scholarly inquiry in American librarianship evolved as a target of more or less concern and action primarily after the first quarter of the twentieth century. However, Shera (1972) notes that because the empirical character of library research, and its excessive dependence upon local observations and limited data, more frequently than not it is provincial and parochial rather than general in applicability. An important thing to note is that research in librarianship is still relatively young. Clear conceptions of the goals, objectives and methodologies of library science research are only now beginning to be solidly formulated. Furthermore, the actual value of research to librarianship still remains in question in various quarters of the field—even though generous lip service to research is widely expressed.

Although some practising librarians may be content to learn and apply conventional, generally accepted library techniques and practices, others realize the value of understanding why various library methods were devised and how knowledge of the field can be further accumulated and expanded. Furthermore, some librarians are now interested in procedures whereby more reliable and valid knowledge is generated for practical use or theoretical considerations. Librarians who purport to function as scientists must formulate ideas or hypotheses about library and information phenomena and test them to gain new insights and knowledge. Lancour (1971) pointed out that it is only through scientific research that librarianship can move out of the condition of being almost exclusively dependent on knowledge acquired in trial-and-error experience into one systematized into scientific laws and theories.

The study of library science as a discipline or professional endeavour has not yet attained full recognition as a legitimate field of scholarship and learning within the academic community at large, an idea that is seen as controversial. Perhaps this lack of recognition by and assimilation in the community of scholars is a product of the slow pace at which librarians have attempted to build a system of theory and to formulate scientific bases for their operations. Certainly, librarians have not been as interested in theoretical considerations as have most scholars in the physical and social sciences. In addition, they have not been very successful in fostering a spirit of inquiry and scientific method in LIS education. According to Gorman (2003), many prestigious research universities in American have given up on LIS education, leading to a diminution of library-related research. This issue has been countered by Dillon and Norris (2005). The most important in their argument is the attention paid to the curriculum. To support their position that the LIS curriculum is responsive to the profession, Dillon and Norris cited the research of Karen Markey who analysed the curricula of 56 North American LIS programmes and found that there are five core course categories in LIS education. According to Dillon and Norris there appears to be a general consensus about what a modern LIS curriculum should contain, at least from the providers' perspective. In addition, Dillon and Norris compared Markey's results with Michael Gorman's recommended core curriculum and found that they are quite similar.

Siegel (1971) conducted an interesting investigation of the prestige of various occupational groups in the USA, including librarians. His study produced one finding that should spur librarians to positive thought and action on a number of fronts, including that of the conduct of scholarly, scientific research and hence fostering of more professionalism within the field. Using the NORC (National Opinion Research Center) Prestige Scale as an instrument, Siegel ranked many occupations according to the esteem they engendered. Librarians received a rank of 55, which coincided with that of sheriffs, actors and statisticians, ranking only a few points higher than funeral directors (52), dieticians (52), locomotive engineers (51) and computer programmers (51). Professionals who attained higher rankings in the study included clergymen (69), dentists (74), lawyers (76), university professors (78) and physicians (82) (Vaughn, 1976). It is likely that many factors were taken into consideration, but some of the problems associated with professional recognition and identity are undoubtedly related to the relative immaturity, with respect to the conduct of research, of the field of librarianship. Indeed, only in the past 50 years have some librarians become concerned about the conduct of library science research; these librarians are still struggling to carve a niche in library science scholarship and learning. In a judgement of the status of research within the field, Paul Wasserman states that at its worst, there is a type of profound negativism that implies that the problems of librarianship are basically unsuited for intellectualization—as if there was a fundamental dichotomy between thought and action, between theory and practice (Wasserman, 1972). With the ongoing controversies that surround the LIS curriculum, this is probably true. Stoffle and Leeder (2005) defend library education as it exists today, stating that there are not enough resources and personnel to support the kind of curricula for which practitioners are asking. They contend that the LIS curricula are doing a great job of providing an education that is general enough to serve as a strong foundation for all librarians. This may be so, but librarianship is still lagging behind other professions in building theoretical knowledge through empirical research.

Conclusions and suggestions

The world has become flatter than what it used to be in generations past. Friedman (2007) believes there should be inspiration for youth to be scientists, engineers and mathematicians. This calls for highly skilled school and college librarians and information scientists. Knowledge of research is important to deliver the kinds of services the new generation of scientists will need. Another major purpose of research is to create new knowledge. The LIS profession needs to advance beyond its heavy dependence on descriptive data and establish principles and theories on which service can be based. If LIS is to maintain its status among other disciplines as a profession rather than a vocation, then the education of future generations of LIS professionals may have to change. This can only improve by the inclusion of mandatory research methods courses in the LIS schools' curricula. In order to foster a culture of research and publication, library professional organizations and societies should encourage the sharing of information through conferences, meetings and roundtables, which are devoted to discussions on research and the conduct of research. Publishers of professional scholarly literature can also encourage research by publishing the results of empirical studies through the commission of articles, books and book chapters.

Continuing education is another way of increasing one's knowledge, and the Association of College and Research Libraries (a division of the American Library Association) offers numerous e-learning opportunities, such as resource sharing, screencasting, electronic collection development of the academic e-library, virtual reference, designing websites for the academic library assessment, and website usability. Other Association of College and Research Libraries courses deal with the management of libraries such as: leading in changing times, mentoring, and the future of higher education. These are necessary learning opportunities so that we can retool for the fast changing digital age.

The 1-year duration of the Master's programme may be inadequate to accommodate research methods courses in addition to the traditional and specialized courses. Perhaps one solution is to have two parallel tracks, the research-oriented track and the practice-oriented track. The research-oriented track will incorporate research methods, design, evaluation and statistical analysis. In the interim, learning opportunities for conducting research are equally important. It may be a challenge, but as the ancient Chinese proverb reminds us, the journey of a thousand miles must begin with a single step.

Overview of the research process

'Research' is a word that is used loosely to mean a variety of activities, such as collecting information on some phenomena and reworking them into new products. However, Leedy (1989) defines it as 'a procedure by which we attempt to find systematically and with the support of demonstrable fact, the answer to a question or the resolution of a problem.' If any of these definitions is true, then the research project, whatever its size or complexity will consist of identifying a question that demands an answer, or a need that requires a resolution. Research projects also consist of defining a research problem, working out how this problem can be investigated, coming to conclusions on the basis of what is found, and reporting the outcome in one form or the other (Walliman, 2005).

Modern research is based on the scientific method of inquiry. Walliman (2005) recognized six characteristics of the scientific method of inquiry: (1) it is generated by a question; (2) it necessitates clarification of a goal; (3) it entails a specific programme of work; (4) it is aimed at increasing understanding by interpreting facts or ideas and reaching some conclusions about their meaning; (5) it requires reasoned argument to support conclusions; and (6) it is iterative in its activities. Resolution of research problems often gives rise to further problems that need resolving. Research is divided into two broad types, basic and applied. The difference between these two broad types of research is worth noting. Basic research includes studies conducted to achieve a fuller understanding of a phenomenon without consideration of how findings will be applied (Busha and Harter, 1980). In other words, it is research driven by a researcher's curiosity or interest. Its main goal is to expand knowledge. Applied research on the other hand, is designed to solve practical problems.

This chapter covers the first five stages of the research process as illustrated in Figure 3.1. The remaining steps of the research process will be discussed in subsequent chapters.

1. Review of the subject area.

2. Finding a problem area.

3. Define the research problem.

4. Review of the literature.

5. Examine ethical issues.

Figure 3.1   **The research process**

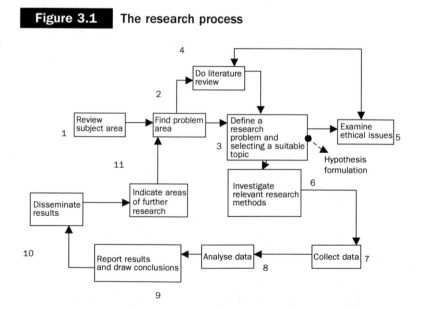

Getting started

With most new projects, getting started with research can be a daunting task. It is normal to feel at a loss as to where to begin or what to do. However, there are survival strategies. Answers to four important questions set the stage for a successful research project.

- *What are you going to do?* The answer to this question will determine the purpose and outcomes that are expected from the research.

- *Why are you doing it?* The answer to this question gives justification for the study. Review of the relevant literature will usually be the best way to tackle this question.

- *How are you going to do it?* You have to lay out a plan of action to show how the problem will be investigated, what data are to be collected, with what methods, and how the information is to be analysed in order to come to conclusions.

- *When are you going to do it?* Constructing a feasible timeline will keep the research on track.

Where to find ideas

The problem under investigation may originate from a library or a situation that is intriguing or as a result of pure intuition. You want to study an area you know very well, but sometimes you might want to study a new area that catches your imagination. In the words of a former colleague, 'it forces me to learn more about that topic.' Librarians are both professionals and practitioners, so the literature is based mostly on practical experience. Through your research reports, you can share details of how you designed and conducted a survey, how you planned and executed an outreach programme, how you wrote, received and expended a grant or any other professional activity.

Another rich source of research ideas is the professional literature. Each research article usually has a recommendation for future research at its conclusion. You can replicate the same study in a different setting and compare the results, or you can elaborate on the study. The Internet is also a rich source of ideas for research. Online communities, blogs, discussion lists and listservs are examples of online interactions that can provide ideas for research. For instance, digitization of rare materials, e-books collections and usage, digital reference, and social networking are some of the topics that could be explored. There will be more suggestions on broad areas of research later in this chapter.

Review of the subject area of interest

One of the key stages in the research process is identifying a suitable problem area by reviewing the literature of the subject of interest. Part of the process of understanding the general problem and its context is that the relevant professional and scholarly literature should be carefully studied. This initial literature review is an important step because it may help to prevent unnecessary research, which occurs if someone repeats research that has been previously conducted.

Identification of the research problem

Problem situations abound around us that may give rise to research. However, three sources usually contribute to problem identification. First, our experience or the experience of others may be the source of a research problem. (For example, one might want to know the effect of information literacy instruction administered to first year students as measured by their scores in general education courses at the end of the year.) Second, the relevant literature in one's field could be another source. Third, the shortcomings in another scholar's theories could be sources of research problems. In identifying a research problem, you must keep the following in mind:

- A clear outline of the general context of the problem area should be given.
- Key theories, concepts and ideas current in this area should be highlighted.
- Assumptions underlying this area must be understood.
- Important issues should be identified.
- What needs to be solved?
- Reading around the subject to know the background and to identify unanswered questions or controversies, and/or to identify the most significant issues for further exploration.

The research problem should be stated in such a way that it could lead to analytical thinking on your part with the aim of offering possible solutions to the stated problem. The research problem could be stated in the form of either a question or a statement, examples are shown as:

- *Example 1—a question*: What is the effect of an online tutorial on a student's performance in general education courses?
- *Example 2—a statement*: The purpose of this study is to find out the effect of an online tutorial on a student's performance in general education courses.

The world is teeming with questions and unresolved problems, but not all of them are suitable research problems. In order for a problem to qualify as a suitable research problem, it must have the following features, and the answers to the questions must be affirmative:

- Does it have current interest to the researcher or to others?

- Is it significant?

- Will the research contribute new information to the body of knowledge and lead to further research?

- Is the research free of ethical problems and limitations?

- Will the information required be accessible?

- Will it be possible for another researcher to replicate the research?

- Will it have value?

- Will you be able to draw conclusions?

Defining the research problem

One can focus on a research problem by finding a broad subject area, narrowing it down to a plausible topic, questioning the topic from several points of view and defining a rationale for the study (Booth *et al.*, 1995). The selection of an appropriate topic is the first step and probably the first major challenge of conducting a research project. Studies have shown that the common mistakes people make when selecting a research topic are:

1. Formulating a research problem that only has the comparison of two or more sets of data. If nothing new is revealed from the exercise, there is no research activity that qualifies to be called a scientific inquiry.

2. Setting up a problem in order to find the degree of correlation between two sets of data. Finding a link between two sets of data does not prove a causal relationship.

3. Devising a study in which the answer is either yes or no. This does not provide a solution to the problem that is being investigated. For example, the question:

- 'Is there a difference between X and Y?' gives a yes or no answer. It does not give the reason why one is different from the other. A better alternative could be 'what is the relationship between X and Y?' This reformulates the inquiry to determine whether the relationship is positive or negative and whether the product of their relationship has an effect on one phenomenon or the other. The following two examples show a good and a bad research topic.
- *Example 1*. A study to show whether the advantages of allowing food in the library outweigh the disadvantages.
- *Example 2*. An analysis of the influence of online tutorials on the performance of first year students.

Which of these two examples is a researchable problem? Obviously, the second one is, because the first one is a description of strengths and weaknesses of a situation, not subjected to a scientific inquiry.

Identifying a research topic

The first stage in a research process is to recognize a need for specific information, pinpointing pertinent phenomena that can be observed, interpreted and evaluated. Thus, the selection of a topic for an inquiry is a key element of the research process. Although experienced researchers are aware of numerous areas that require original or replicated research, novices may be frustrated in their efforts to focus on a specific question. Owing to the interdisciplinary nature of librarianship and the broad scope of the profession, numerous library science topics are appropriate for exploration. We must always make choices that appeal to our own interests, curiosity and current knowledge. If you decide to study the use of citation analysis in collection management, for instance, you should make that decision because you are interested in the issue, know something about it already, and/or would like to know more about it. However, because we rarely study solely for our own satisfaction, we must consider matters other than our own interests as we choose topics.

Finding a topic and posing a relevant research question represent the important initial steps in the conduct of a research project. A well chosen topic can lead to the types of research questions that fuel your academic interests for years to come. At the very least, though, topics can be seen as occasions for making your research relevant and meaningful to your own personal and academic concerns. Before choosing and narrowing a topic to investigate, consider why you want to study it and who will benefit from it. Your audience often dictates the types of topics that are favourable for investigation. For instance, practising librarians in 2009 will be interested in the perception of the 'digital natives' of the usefulness of the library website.

In the workplace, purpose and audience are often defined for you. For instance, you might have to describe your experience with a particular instructional session to a co-worker, outlining the flaws. In this case, your purpose and audience are obvious, and your topic is equally evident. A student may have to work a little harder to determine which topics are appropriate for particular purposes and audiences.

Sources of research topics

Suggestions for future research are usually stated at the end of scholarly research articles, theses and dissertations. These are rich sources of ideas for research. An example appeared in the article by Knievel *et al.* in *College and Research Libraries* published in 2006. The study examined the use of circulation

Table 3.1	Suggested areas and sub-areas for research

Library as a place
    Use and non-use of the physical building
    Who uses the library and for what purpose?
    Food and drink in the library
    Library cafes
Library website
    Usability studies of the Online Public Access Catalog (OPAC)
        How do users search the catalogue?
        What errors occur while searching and why?
        How effective are subject headings?
Usability studies of online databases
    How do users construct their searches?
        Basic search
        Advanced search
        Do they use wildcards?
        Do they use cross-search?
    What is the difference between searches in Google and searches in library databases?
Collections
    What are the perceptions of collection librarians on the effectiveness of collection development policies?
    Using citation analysis as a collection development tool
    Comparative collection analysis for collection assessment and evaluation
    Interlibrary loan records as collection development and management tool
    Advantages and disadvantages of on-site and off-site storage facilities
        Studies to identify criteria to be used as guides to determine when materials should be retired to storage
    Consortia
    Access versus ownership
    Vendor selection process
    Licensing
    Formats, electronic or print, which and why?
    Journal packages and aggregators how effective are they?
    Collections budget
    Electronic books—access and use
Availability of materials
    How can the need for duplicate copies of library materials be predicted?
        Interlibrary loan—perception of effectiveness
Weeding
    Studies to define criteria for weeding a collection
Digital projects
    Electronic theses and dissertations
    Institutional repositories
    Rare book digitization and finding aids
Circulation studies
    What circulates?
    How does circulation relate to benefits for the library community?
    Effect of different loan periods on availability of materials
    How effective are library fines as deterrents to overdue books?
    What is the effect of closed stacks on the research process?
Catalogue record
    What should be included (particularly in view of the digital age)
    What bibliographic characteristics of library materials do the users tend to remember and use?
Microform
    What are unique problems of microform usage in libraries?
    Evaluation of microform collections and services

statistics and interlibrary loan data in collection management. At the end of their study, the authors stated that 'Although the literature includes many studies utilizing circulation statistics or interlibrary loan data, very few published studies investigate the intersection of circulation, interlibrary loan, and holdings, an intersection that can provide very fruitful guidance for subject librarians' (Knievel *et al.*, 2006).

A list of suggested general topics is given in Table 3.1.

Hypothesis formulation

Another step in the research process is formulating a hypothesis, which is defined as a tentative assumption made in order to draw out and test its logical or empirical consequences (Merriam Webster, 2001). Hypotheses may also be referred to as hunches or reasonable guesses made in the form of statements about a cause or situation (Walliman, 2005). For example, if statistics show that the number of questions received at the reference desk has decreased considerably, we might hypothesize that information literacy instruction reduces reference inquiries. For each hypothesis, a particular action taken could support or reject it. If a hypothesis is supported then there is a good chance that one can act to remedy the problem. For instance, if it is supported that the information literacy instruction reduces reference inquiries, then the library can direct more resources into that venture.

Hypothesis is not always appropriate for all research topics, but if one uses it in research, it must arise naturally from the research problem and appear to the reader to be reasonable and sound. There are two grounds on which a hypothesis may be justified as logical and empirical. First, logical justification is developed from arguments based on concepts, theories and premises relating directly to the research problem. Second, empirical justification is based on reference to other research found in the literature (Walliman, 2005). Where hypotheses are not appropriate, there are other forms in which the research problem can be expressed to indicate the method of investigation. They could be stated in the form of a question or questions? (*Example*: How do students perceive the library's efforts to improve group study areas?) They could be in the form of research statements. (*Example*: A study of the influence of an in-house coffee shop on the use of collections and services.)

Hypotheses can also be stated in the form of null hypothesis and alternative hypothesis. A positive result will result in rejection of the null hypothesis and a negative result will result in failing to reject the null hypothesis.

- *Example 1—null hypothesis*: there is no relationship between information literacy instruction and reference desk inquiries.

- *Example 2—alternative hypothesis*: there is a relationship between information literacy instruction and reference desk inquiries.

Hypotheses can also be directional or non-directional. In directional hypotheses, a direction is specified, such as greater than, less than, positively and negatively. In non-directional hypotheses, the direction is not specified.

- *Example of a directional hypothesis*: at the end of the first year, students who attended the freshman seminar will have higher grade point averages than those who did not.

- *Example of a non-directional hypothesis*: at the end of the first year, there will be a difference in the grade point average of the students who attended the freshman seminar and those who did not.

Review of current literature

In the research process, the literature review stands as the pivotal point of all activities. Everything hinges on theories, concepts and past research and awareness of current issues that can be unleashed by an extensive review of the literature. A literature review is defined as a selection of available documents, published or unpublished, on the topic of interest. Furthermore, it is the effective evaluation of these documents in relation to the research being proposed (Hart, 1998).

A good quality literature review has appropriate breadth and depth, rigour and consistency, clarity and brevity, and effective analysis and synthesis. In other words, the researcher uses ideas in the literature to justify the particular approach, or the selection of methods, and demonstrates that the research contributes something new. Furthermore, a good one plays out a dialogue between the writer and reader, with the reader asking questions like 'What is your point here?' 'What makes you think so?' 'So what?' The more the writer can anticipate these questions, the easier it will be to formulate the arguments (Rudestam and Newton, 2007). 'Where are you going with this?' is a good question a researcher must ask himself.

In writing the literature review, the introduction must have explicitly stated the goals and structure of the evolving argument. The purpose of the literature review is to test your research question(s) against that which is already known. Your literature review should answer several questions:

- What is known?
- Is there a consensus on relevant issues?
- Is there significant debate on issues? What are the various positions?

- Is there an important chronology to the development of knowledge that affects the questions you are asking?

- What are the gaps in knowledge? Which gaps have been identified by other researchers? Which gaps are apparent from your review and how do you intend to fill them?

- What appears to be the most fruitful research directions? Which directions have been indicated by other researchers? Which directions do you see as a result of your literature review?

One common problem among new scholars is deferring to the authority of others in the review. A preferable strategy is to develop a theme and then cite the work of relevant authors to buttress the argument (Rudenstam and Newton, 2007). Apart from these overall questions, for a critical review, you must ask yourself some specific questions concerning each citation you include in your literature review. You must ask questions about whether the author formulated and clearly defined the problem; whether his approach was effective; or whether he could have examined it from another perspective. Other important questions include what the research orientation of the author was, was it interpretive or critical science, or what his theoretical framework was. In reading each article or book, you must assess whether the author covered the relevant literature of the problem, particularly those covering opposing viewpoints. In addition, was the research design appropriate and was the analysis of the data accurate? Were the conclusions based on the data and analysis? Did the author specify the limitations of the study? Most important of all, does it relate to the specific premise of your own research? If the literature review is done properly, then at the end of it the reader should be convinced that your study needs to be carried out at this point in time to move knowledge in this area forward.

Other benefits of literature reviews are that they: help to narrow and to more clearly delineate the research problem; reveal overlooked conclusions and facts that ought to be taken into consideration before a research study is actually initiated; suggest new approaches to the planning of the investigation; uncover methodologies that were used successfully by other researchers; help in the determination of the degree to which particular problems have already been investigated; and assist investigators to develop firmer understandings of theoretical implications of proposed inquiries (Bush and Harter, 1980, p. 19).

Database searching

Post-1950s, researchers had to search print indexes because there were limited or no electronically generated ones. This was a tedious and time-consuming exercise that could prolong the research process significantly. With the advent of the Internet and the World Wide Web, searching the literature became much easier. The most notable bibliographic databases in the area of library and information science are: *Library Literature and Information Science*, and *Library and Information Science Abstracts* (*LISA*). Both of these databases are proprietary and they do carry a subscription but most libraries have one or the other. As electronic journals are now more prevalent than printed ones, these databases also have links to full text articles. Another related database is a free resource, Education Resource Information Center (ERIC). ERIC provides free access to more than 1.2 million bibliographic records of journal articles and other education-related materials and, if available, includes links to full text. ERIC is sponsored by the US Department of Education, Institute of Education Sciences (IES). This database can be accessed from http://www.eric.ed.gov/.

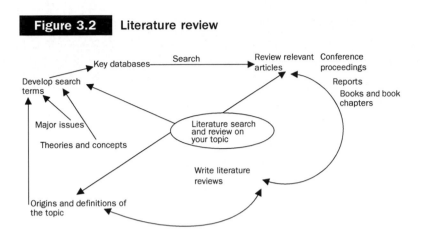

Figure 3.2 Literature review

Library literature and information science

This database can be a valuable resource for your literature review. It indexes English and foreign-language periodicals, selected state journals, conference proceedings, pamphlets, books and book chapters, and library school theses and dissertations. It indexes over 400 periodicals dating back to 1984; many of which are peer reviewed. It covers feature articles and delivers full text articles in PDF (Portable Document Format) format, from over 100 select publications. It also steers users to valuable information on the Web by linking to the sites mentioned in the articles. It helps users keep up with the latest concepts, trends, opinions, theories and methodologies in the areas of library and information science. Subject areas covered include: automation, care and restoration of books, cataloguing, censorship, circulation procedures, classification, copyright education for librarianship, electronic searching, government aid indexing, information brokers, Internet software, library associations and conferences, library equipment and supplies, literature for children and young adults, personnel administration, preservation of materials, public relations, publishing, rare books, reference services and Web Sites (Wilson, 2008). Here are some suggestions on how you can search it effectively.

Always utilize the 'advanced search' strategy so that you can customize your search, eliminate irrelevant records and save time. An example is given in Figure 3.3.

Figure 3.3 **Samples of advanced searches**

> **SAMPLES OF ADVANCED SEARCHES**
>
> *Searching for an interview with library directors on personnel?*
>
> a. Enter 'library directors' as your All-Smart Search.
> b. Choose 'Interview' from the **Document Type** dropdown box.
> c. Choose **Relevance** in the **Sort By** dropdown, to view the most relevant record.
>
> *Want to find books on the criteria for weeding?*
>
> a. Enter 'Weeding' as your All-Smart Search.
> b. Type 'criteria' in the second All Smart Search box
> c. Choose 'Books' from the **Document Type** dropdown menu.
> d. Choose **Date** in the **Sort By** dropdown menu to view the latest record first.

Figure 3.4 **Searching library literature**

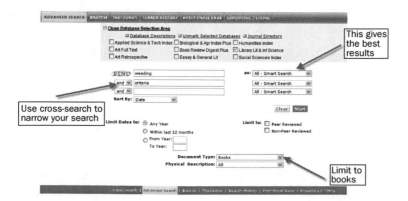

The searches shown in Figure 3.4 are from the Wilson's database. Other vendors' database search may differ, but they generally have the same principles.

Ethical issues

Background

In conducting research, particularly with human subjects, abiding by ethical standards is very important. In the past, ethics was not taken seriously. Between 1930 and 1972, the US Public Health Service (USPHS) was treating African American men infected with syphilis in the southern states of the country. Funding for this project dried up as the Depression set in. As a result, the PHS decided to conduct an experiment on the effect of untreated syphilis in living humans. The experiment was conducted in Tuskegee, Alabama. They enrolled 399 poor, mostly illiterate, male African American sharecroppers infected with syphilis, since there was a debate about the racial variation in the effects of syphilis. Individuals enrolled in the study were not required to give informed consent and were not informed of their diagnosis. Instead, they received free health examinations, rides to the clinic, meals and burial insurance in case of death in return for participating. They were not treated or treated minimally, at first with low doses then medication was replaced with 'pink stuff' (aspirin), so that they were not cured. The Tuskegee Syphilis Study was one of the most horrendous examples of research carried out in disregard of basic ethical principles of conduct. By the time the study was shut down, 28 of the men had died of syphilis, 100 were dead of related complications, 40 of their wives had been infected, and 19 of their children had been born with congenital syphilis. The publicity surrounding the study was one of the major influences leading to the codification of protection of human subjects in research.

On 12 July 1974, the National Research Act (Pub.L.93–348) was signed into law, thereby creating the National Commission for the Protection of Human Subjects of Biomedical and Behavioral Research. The commission was charged to identify the basic principles that should underlie the conduct of research using human subjects and to develop guidelines that should be followed to assure that such research is conducted according to those principles.

Belmont Report

The Belmont Report attempts to summarize the basic ethical principles identified by the commission in 1976. The Belmont Report describes three fundamental principles:

1. *Respect for persons.* This is divided into two separate requirements. First, is that individuals should have autonomy and should be treated as autonomous agents. Second, individuals with diminished autonomy are entitled to protection. The autonomous person is an individual who is capable of deliberation about personal goals. To respect an autonomous person is to give weight to the person's opinion and choices while refraining from obstructing his actions unless it is detrimental to others. To show lack of respect is to ignore that person's considered judgements, to deny an individual the freedom to act on those judgements, or to withhold information that enables him to make a considered judgement when there are compelling reasons to do so. The persons in the second group, those with diminished autonomy are those who lack the capacity for self-determination either due to immaturity

or loss of mental acuity. These need protection and the extent of protection should depend upon the risk of harm and the likelihood of benefit. In this category are children, the elderly, mentally disabled and the ill. Those incarcerated are also included in this category because the conditions in the prison are controlling and individuals may be subtly coerced or unduly influenced.

2. *Beneficence*. A person's welfare is strictly adhered to, which is to do no harm and maximize possible benefits while minimizing harms.

3. *Justice*. An injustice occurs when some benefits that a person is entitled are denied without good reason or when some burden is imposed unduly. Widely accepted formulations of just ways to distribute burdens and benefits are as follows: (a) to each person an equal share; (b) to each person according to individual need; (c) to each person according to individual effort; (d) to each person according to societal contribution; and (e) to each person according to merit.

In 1997, 65 years after the experiment started, President Bill Clinton apologized to the survivors of the Tuskegee Syphilis Study.

Against this historical background, ethical concern in scientific inquiry requiring interaction with humans is a critical component of the review and approval of the research protocols. Any research involving surveys, interviews or experimental research involving human beings falls into this category. Those involving secondary data, meaning data that have been previously collected by someone else, need no formal review by the Institutional Review Board (IRB). Busha and Harter (1980) presented some general principles that are widely accepted in the scientific community as fundamentals of the inquiry process and are regarded as ethical benchmarks. These principles include the following:

- Do not misrepresent the investigative competencies and abilities of the researcher or associates.

- Protect human subjects by taking all possible measures to respect privacy and the confidentiality of personalized research data.

- Follow the principle of full disclosure of intent to subjects.

- Report procedures and findings as accurately as possible.

- Give credit to persons whose earlier research was especially useful in the conduct of your research.

- Give credit to research associates who provided direct assistance.

- Acknowledge the aid of persons who served as consultants or who helped to plan, conduct or report research activities.

- If applicable, acknowledge sources of financial grants and other forms of direct or indirect aid.

- Always place a high value on intellectual honesty.

Before you can begin collecting data of any kind using any form of data collection tool, you have to obtain the approval of the IRB of your institution. IRB (or other body responsible for protecting the interest of human subjects in research) oversees the ethical compliance in human subject research. The process of IRB approval is complex and time consuming, but it is a necessary step if the research is to be published or made public in any form. Most institutions have information about the application for IRB approval on their web sites. (Example: http://www.research.vcu.edu/forms/irb.htm). The earlier you sought this out and gained knowledge of the rules and procedures the better. Make sure the consent of research subjects is obtained.

Informed consent

One of the most important ethical rules governing research on humans is that participants must give their informed consent before taking part in a study. Most IRBs require that each participant be informed of the following:

- Who is conducting the research?
- Why was the participant chosen?
- What is the time commitment?
- What is the reward for participants? Any benefits?
- Any potential risks and how can they be protected?
- What the study is about?
- Participation is voluntary.
- Listen to any concerns and answer any questions.

Once all these have been done, the participants should sign an 'Informed Consent Form'. Further information summarizing the essential elements of informed consent according to the US Government can be found at: http://www.socialpsychology.org/consent.htm/.

Other ethical issues

There are other ethical issues such as:

- *Privacy*: control over the data, against sharing protected information or receiving unwanted information, must be maintained at all times.
- *Confidentiality*: agreements about what will be done and may not be done with the data should be made; this may include legal constraints.
- *Anonymity*: identifiers, information that would indicate which individuals or organizations provide which data,

must be removed from all data before making results of the research public.

- *Security of the data must be maintained*. The researcher has the obligation to use the data appropriately, without doing any harm or wrong. A pledge to this effect must be given to the participants.

- *Debriefing*: this is an important ethical issue that is often omitted by researchers. Typically, all participants deserve to have the opportunity to learn about the results of the study. It is necessary to let participants know how the debriefing will be done. It could be by giving a description of the purpose of the research in detail or by sending a summary of the results to those who may want it.

Conclusions

The research process starts with reviewing a subject area of interest and identifying a problem area, defining a problem, selecting a topic and then doing a literature review. The latter is an important task of identifying relevant literature to buttress the themes that you develop for your research. You can find ideas in your daily practice or in any area of the profession that interests you. It has been said in professional circles that early career librarians should pick a theme that can fuel their enthusiasm, focusing on that as they grow in the profession. However, it may be as beneficial to be identified with a specific theme as to be varied and diverse in your research. Whichever works for you, the key is to be able to translate research into practice.

4

Research designs

Chapter 3 gave an overview of the research process, with a description of the first five steps. This chapter will focus on research designs. Design as used in research refers to the plan the researcher lays down on how to proceed with the research. Research can be categorized as qualitative and quantitative. In quantitative research, problem statements or research questions have to be concise and unambiguous. Qualitative research attempts to obtain a more holistic impression of the research problem. Important part of the problem statement is the information on the variables that will be investigated.

Variables

A variable may be thought of as any property of a person, thing, event, setting and so on that is not fixed (Marshall, 1989). Variables can be perceived or labelled in a variety of ways depending on the nature of the relationship between or among them. For instance, in a causal relationship, the variable identified first in the hypothesis is referred to as the independent variable. An independent variable can also be called the predictor variable or experimental variable. An independent variable is that which influences or causes changes in the other main factor (Powell and Connaway, 2004). The second main factor in the causal hypothesis is referred to as the dependent variable. This variable represents the measure that reflects the outcomes of a research study, the variable that is influenced by the independent variable. Variables can be ordinal, categorical, continuous or interval.

Ordinal variable

Ordinal variables rank data in terms of degree. They do not establish the numeric difference between data points. For example, letter grades A, B, C and D are nominal. The rank is: A higher than B, B higher than C, and C higher than D, but the precise numeric difference between each letter grade is not known.

Categorical variable

Categorical variable is one that has two or more categories but no ordering to the categories. For example, gender is a categorical variable (male and female). Hair colour is another one (blonde, brunette, red, brown, etc.).

Continuous variable

If the values of a variable can be divided into fractions, it is called continuous variable. Such a variable can take infinite numbers of values. For example, test scores, age, income or temperatures.

Interval variable

Interval variables are similar to ordinal variable except that the intervals between the values of the interval variables are equally spaced, for example, income of persons A, B and C are, $10,000, $20,000 and $30,000 respectively. The difference of $10,000 exists between each person.

Extraneous variables

A basic problem in research is that there are other possible variables that could affect the dependent variable unknown to the researcher. These variables are known as extraneous variables and they can bias results of the study. Extraneous variables are independent variables that have not been controlled. The task for the researcher is to control these extraneous variables to eliminate their effect. Extraneous variables can be classified into three types corresponding to the type of independent variable they affect. Subject extraneous variables are characteristics of the subject being studied that might affect the way they behave. These variables could include gender, age, sex, race, etc. Experimental extraneous variables are the characteristics of the person conducting the research that might influence how a person behaves. These could include gender and language proficiency. Situational extraneous variables are features of the environment in which the research is conducted that may affect the outcome of the study in a negative way. Included in this category are air quality, lighting, humidity, temperature and time of day. One way to control extraneous variables is to hold them constant. For instance, if a researcher includes only boys as subjects of a study, he is controlling for the subject extraneous variable of gender. Another way of controlling extraneous variables is to balance them in the group.

Quantitative methods

As stated earlier, quantitative designs are those in which research questions are concise, unambiguous and preset. A common quantitative design is experimental design. A simple example of experimental design is the one in which two groups of subjects are randomly selected from a population and one group (the experimental group) receives a treatment and the other group (the control group) receives no treatment. At the end of the experiment, both groups are tested to see if there is a difference on a specified test score. The experimental design is subdivided into true experimental, pre-experimental and quasi-experimental. These types were made famous by Campbell and Stanley (1963). This book focuses on true experimental, with a brief discussion of pre-experimental and quasi-experimental designs.

Experimental designs

True experimental design

In experimental research, independent variable is manipulated; hence it is called experimental variable or treatment variable. The variable that it affects, the dependent variable is called the outcome variable. Experimental designs have certain characteristics that distinguish them from other research methods. These include:

- statistical equivalence of subjects in different groups
- comparison of two or more groups or sets of conditions
- direct manipulation of at least one independent variable
- measurement of each dependent variable
- use of inferential statistics
- the researcher strives to isolate and control every relevant condition that determines the events investigated, so as to observe the effects when the conditions are manipulated.

In order to make the groups equivalent, random assignment to groups is necessary. Random assignment is the use of chance procedures in experiments to ensure that each participant has equal opportunity to be assigned to any given group. In addition to subjects, an experimental design involves a control group that is not subjected to the experiment. The purpose of the control group is to serve as a comparison. A control group is the key to experimental design and is the feature that distinguishes it from other research methods. In its simplest, an experiment involves making a change in the value of one variable—called the independent variable—and observing the effect of that change on another variable—called the dependent variable (Cohen and Manion, 2000).

True experimental design is one in which the subjects are randomly assigned to groups and the independent variables are manipulated to detect their effect on the dependent variable. This technique is used where there is time priority in a causal relationship, i.e. cause precedes effect. Because experimental design deals with cause and effect, it must have validity to determine whether the experiment makes a difference.

For a detailed discussion on experimental designs, see Fraenkel and Wallen (2006) and McMillan (2008).

It is possible to investigate more than one independent and (also more than one dependent variable) in a study. For simplicity's sake, I will present an example of a study in which only one independent and one dependent variable are involved. In a study to investigate the effect of information literacy on student learning, information literacy is the independent variable and student learning (measured by scores or grades) is the dependent variable.

- *Example 1: research statement.* Students whose curriculum includes information literacy instruction have a better academic outcome (GPA) than students whose curriculum does not.

In order to find out whether information literary instruction has any effect on academic performance, an experimental research was conducted on 50 randomly selected students from the population. One of the unique characteristics of true experimental research is that the subjects are randomly assigned, that is, every individual who is participating in the experiment has an equal chance of being assigned to any of the experimental or control conditions that are being compared. The subjects are randomly assigned to either a treatment group A or the control group B. Group A had information literacy instruction, and group B, had no information literacy instruction. At the end of the semester the academic performance measured by GPA (dependent variable) of group A was compared with those of group B students. The results showed that group A performed better than group B. Having controlled for all other factors that could influence the results, it was concluded that the cause of the better performance was the information literary instruction.

Complete equivalence between experimental and control groups can seldom be obtained in research in the social sciences (Busha and Harter, 1980) because of numerous environmental and hereditary factors that cannot normally be known. Then at best equivalence can only be approximate.

- *Example 2: Hypothesis.* High school students who study a unit of instruction in library skills in conjunction with coursework in other subjects such as history or English literature learn library skills more effectively than high school students who study an equivalent unit independently of other school subjects.

To test this hypothesis, there are certain variables that need to be controlled. The two groups of students should be roughly equivalent in levels of motivation, intelligence, socio-economic status, age and other qualities. This is because any of these variables might have a differential effect on otherwise equivalent students. For example, if the students of group A manifest more collective intelligence than group B, then that factor itself may cause students in group A to learn library skills more effectively than those in group B. However, by designing an experiment so the two groups are roughly equivalent in intelligence, this variable is controlled, and thus the effect should be the same for both groups (Busha and Harter, 1980, p. 37). This is achieved by random assignment of the randomly selected sample. A random selection of 30 participants from the population was randomly assigned to group I (treatment group) and group II (control group); group I was assigned to the class that had the library instruction in conjunction with coursework in social studies and group II was assigned to the class that had library instruction independently of another subject. At the end of the session, a test was administered. Results showed that the group that had the library instruction in conjunction with social studies scored higher. The hypothesis was accepted.

Because of the careful control that is exercised in its use, experimental method is the most appropriate technique for investigating causal relationships. By controlling all independent variables, except the treatment variable, the differential effect on the dependent variable in the experimental and control groups, can be said to have been caused by the independent variable.

Pretest post-test control group design

This design randomly assigns the subjects to the experimental group or the control group and gives a pretest to each group on the dependent variable before the treatment. The treatment is applied to the experimental group and none to the control group, then a post-test is given after the treatment. The scores of the pretest are then compared with those of the post-test.

Post-test-only control group design

Post-test-only design is another type of true experimental design that uses the same group of subjects or same set of conditions. Everything is the same as true experimental design except that it does not have a pretest. This design is used when it is not convenient to administer a pretest.

Pre-experimental research

Unlike true experimental design, pre-experimental design does not have random selection of participants from a population, nor do they include a control group. Hence the power of the research to uncover the causal nature of the relationship between independent and dependent variables is greatly reduced. These designs also have little or no control over extraneous variables that may influence the outcome instead of the variable that the researcher intended.

Quasi-experimental design

The quasi-experimental design differs from true experimental and pre-experimental designs in one important way. It does not include random assignment. Researchers who employ these designs rely instead on other techniques to control (or at least reduce) threats to internal validity. Refer to Salkind (2009) and Fraenkel and Wallen (2006) for a detailed account of experimental designs.

Non-experimental design

Non-experimental research methods explore research questions without manipulating a variable. Types of non-experimental design are:

- descriptive research
- survey research
- historical research
- case studies.

Descriptive research

Characteristics of descriptive research

Descriptive research describes the data and characteristics of the phenomenon being studied. It answers the questions, who, what, where, when and how? Though descriptive research could be accurate and systematic, it cannot be used to find a causal relationship. Data for many descriptive studies comprise of newly generated data rather than prerecorded data. Controlled conditions are not used to initiate the occurrence of a desired event. Direct observations of library phenomena offer excellent opportunities for investigators to acquire new data. In addition, the data collection procedures used in descriptive research may be very explicit. Some observation instruments, for example, employ highly refined categories of behaviour and yield quantitative (numerical) data.

Descriptive research may focus on individual subjects and go into depth and detail describing them. Individual variation is allowed and studied. This approach is called a case study (see later, this chapter). Because it can employ data collection techniques such as surveys, it is capable of investigating large groups of subjects as well.

Survey research

The survey is a group of research methods commonly used to determine the present status of a given phenomenon (Powell and Connaway, 2004). The basic assumption of most survey research is that, by carefully following certain scientific procedures, one can obtain an empirical knowledge of a contemporary nature. This knowledge allows generalizations to be made about characteristics, opinions, beliefs, attitudes and so on of the entire population being studied. For example, if one wanted to learn the perceptions of all teaching faculties in the USA regarding electronic journals, one could study a sample of several hundred teaching faculties and use their responses as the basis for estimating the opinion of all teaching faculties in the USA. Unlike experimental research, survey research does not enable the researcher to manipulate the independent variable and provides less control of the research environment. It is therefore not capable of establishing causal relationships.

Librarians have long conducted surveys. Library surveys are associated with attempts to gather information about many aspects of libraries whatever setting these institutions might be located. Survey research methods are the most suitable techniques to determine:

1. How the academic community perceives the adequacy of the library collections?

2. Whether the library facility is seen as a comfortable place by users?

3. Whether the public services are efficient and effective?

4. Attitudes and opinions of library users about the library web sites.

The main way in which information is collected is through asking questions. The answers to these questions by the research participants (sample) constitute the data of the study. The techniques of collecting data are discussed in the next chapter.

Types of surveys

Researchers use two main types of surveys: cross-sectional surveys and longitudinal surveys. In cross-sectional survey research, information is collected from a sample selected from a predetermined population and information is collected at just one point in time. For example, information could be collected from a day to a few weeks' duration, but it is a one time exercise (timeline: data gathering 1–21 April). In a longitudinal survey on the other hand, information is collected at different points in time in order to study changes over time.

Steps in survey research

The steps in survey research are practically the same for most quantitative research. First, you define the problem. Because surveys are usually self-administered, it is important to choose a topic interesting enough to motivate the individuals in the study to respond. A dull uninteresting topic may generate a high percentage of non-response. The second and third steps are to identify the target population from which to choose the sample. The fourth step is to choose an appropriate data collection technique. These could be mail surveys, telephone surveys or personal interviews. After the data are collected, the last steps are to analyse the data and write the report.

Historical research

Historical research is a non-experimental research method that focuses on the evaluation and synthesis of evidence in order to establish facts and draw conclusions about past events. It involves exploring the meaning and relationship of events. It attempts to find out what happened in the past and to reveal reasons for why and how things happened. Simply put, it makes people aware of what has happened in the past so they may learn from past failures and successes. Its resource is primary historical data in the form of artefacts, relics, records and writings. Historical research has some values. For instance, it enables solutions to contemporary problems to be sought in the past as well as throws light on present and future trends. It stresses the relative importance and the effects of the interactions that are found within all cultures. In addition, it allows for the re-evaluation of data supporting selected hypotheses, theories and generalizations that are presently held about the past (Hill and Kerber, 1967). Some aspects of historical research that help determine the scope are: where the events take place, which people are involved, when the events occurred and what kind of human activity was involved. For example, a researcher may use artefacts, archaeological findings and archival records to trace the history of the printed book from generations past.

Researchers undertake historical research for a variety of reasons:

- To learn how things were done in the past to see if they might be applicable to present-day problems.

- To assist in decision making. If a particular idea or approach had been tried before, even under different circumstances, past results may offer policy makers some ideas about how current plans may turn out.

- To study trends of a phenomenon over different periods of time. For example, a researcher may want to study how a literature review was done in the print medium.

Other examples of questions that can be pursued through historical research are:

- How were bibliographic instructions changed in the past 40 years?

- How had access to library collections changed in the last two centuries?

- How had the reference service to physical disabled persons changed in the past 50 years?

- How were the policies and practices of library administration in the early twentieth century different from those of today?

Steps in historical research

Steps in historical research are much the same as in any other form of research: (1) the researcher defines a topic or a problem he wishes to investigate; (2) he formulates a hypothesis; (3) he gathers data from a variety of sources; (4) he evaluates the data for authenticity and accuracy; (5) the data are synthesized or integrated to make a coherent body of information; and (6) the results are interpreted in light of the hypothesis formulated at the beginning of the research.

Sources of historical data

Sources of historical research could be primary or secondary sources. Primary source are ones prepared by individuals who were participants or direct witnesses of the event being described. They are the original artefacts, records, recordings of oral histories, interviews, letters, original manuscripts, diaries, accounting ledgers, deeds and wills, architectural drawings of buildings, and photographs. In short, primary data are still in their original form. Secondary sources are those that have been repackaged from its original form, or interpreted into another form of publication, such as newspaper or an encyclopaedia entry. Something gets lost during the process of transformation. Accuracy may also be in question. As a result, whenever possible, researchers want to use primary rather than secondary sources. Unfortunately, primary sources are admittedly more difficult to obtain, especially the further back in time a researcher searches. Secondary sources are therefore used quite extensively in historical research even though primary sources are preferred.

Digital sources

The digital age is no barrier to conducting historical research. Digital archives of texts abound complete with pathfinders. As digitizing does not change the content in any way, these can still be regarded as primary sources. Also, rare books that have passed into public domain are rich sources of free digital historical documents. In the fast moving world it is not unusual for important primary sources of data to be overlooked. The Digital Natives for instance, may not be interested in preserving historical data now but if the sources are not properly preserved or archived, historical research may be almost impossible to do if and when they later become interested in historical research.

Evaluating historical data

Researchers can never be confident about the genuineness and accuracy of historical sources. Therefore, a historical researcher must adopt a critical attitude toward any and all sources of the reviews. Two criteria are used to review historical documents, external criticism, concerned with authenticity and internal criticism, concerned with accuracy. In external criticism, questions asked include:

- Who wrote the document?
- Were the documents written when they were claimed to be?
- For what purpose?
- Under what conditions?
- Do different forms or versions of the document exist?

Questions asked in internal criticism include:

- Was the author present at the event?
- Was the author a participant or an observer?
- Was the author competent to describe the event?
- Do the contents make sense?

Data analysis in historical research

Data are organized into categories for a content analysis. Researchers pay attention to patterns and themes that emerge and then some coding is done to organize the information along the coding categories.

Limitations of historical research

There are some unique limitations to historical research compared with other research methods. First, because the availability of data is always limited by factors that are not under the control of the researcher, results will most likely be limited in generalizability. Second, historical research is often long and arduous requiring weeks and months pouring over documents as you look for clues and hints to support your hypotheses. Third, historical research data are often questioned because they are primarily derived from the observations of others.

Case studies

Case study is a method used to study an individual, an institution, or a phenomenon in a unique setting in an intense and as detailed a manner as possible. Case studies are a major part of research methodology used by physicians. In medicine, researchers regularly study cases of individuals whose conditions are so unusual that their symptoms and treatment demand special attention and information about their cases need to be disseminated. In business, researchers study cases of businesses that fail as well as those that succeed. In librarianship, Paris (1990) conducted a case study research of library school closings. In each case, the researcher may gain a sharpened understanding of why the instance happened as it did and what might be important to look at more extensively in future research.

Advantages of the case study method

First, because it focuses on only one thing, it enables a very close examination and scrutiny and the collection of a great deal of data. Second, case studies can utilize several different techniques to get the necessary information. They can be based on any mix of quantitative and qualitative evidence, hence, they should not be confused with qualitative research. Third, they lend themselves to generating and testing hypotheses.

Disadvantages of the case study method

The case study method may provide some very important information that could not have been revealed any other way but it does have its shortcomings. First, the researcher has to collect data in a variety of settings, under a variety of conditions for which the researcher has no control over.

Second, case studies lack breadth even though they provide depth. Although they are extremely focused, they are not comprehensive as other research methods. Third, generalizability of the findings from case studies is limited.

Qualitative research methods

Qualitative research methods are appropriate when the phenomena under study are complex, are social in nature and do not lend themselves to quantification (Liebscher, 1998). Qualitative research focuses on attempting to understand why participants react as they do (Mellon, 1986). Qualitative researchers are especially interested in how things occur. Hence, they are likely to observe how people interact with each other; how certain kinds of questions are answered; the meanings that people give to certain words and actions; how people's attitudes are translated into actions (Fraenkel and Wallen, 2006).

General characteristics of qualitative research methods

Qualitative research method explores the processes that underlie human behaviour using techniques such as interviews, observations and case studies. In qualitative research, the natural setting is the direct source of data and the researcher is the key instrument. Qualitative data are collected in the form of words or pictures rather than numbers. Qualitative researchers are concerned with the process as well as the product. Qualitative and quantitative research methods are two different paradigms. Table 4.1 shows the fundamental differences between the two paradigms.

Table 4.1   Quantitative versus qualitative research

Quantitative methodology	Qualitative methodology
Has precise hypotheses	Hypotheses emerge as study develops
Data are numerical	Prefers narrative description
Reliability of scores is critical	Assumes reliability of inference is adequate
Assessment of validity through statistical indices	Assessment of validity through cross-checking sources of information
Random sampling	Purposive samples
Specific design control for bias	Researcher control of procedural bias
Statistical analysis and summary of results	Narrative summary of results
Breaks down complex phenomena into specific parts for analysis	Holistic description of complex phenomena
Could manipulate conditions in studying complex phenomena	Does not tamper with naturally occurring phenomena
Precise description of procedures	Narrative literary description of procedures

In general, the research process is described as a series of clearly defined stages: planning, design, implementation, analysis and conclusions. This linear process applies mostly to quantitative studies in which step-by-step detailed planning is essential even though in reality it does not really proceed in such a clear-cut manner. Qualitative research, on the other hand, tends to be represented as a cyclical process or a series of overlapping stages. Qualitative researchers seek to be open to the setting and subjects of their study allowing this to inform the process and to modify general research plans (Gorman and Clayton, 2005). Essentially, qualitative researchers allow their plans to evolve as they learn more about the subjects and settings.

Though qualitative research is cyclic in nature, it also needs to move forward toward a finite end. Gorman and Clayton call this a pyramid approach. The pyramid starts at the bottom with preliminary preparation, moves into broad exploration and then concentrates on a set of focused activities. The goal is to work up the pyramid, from generalities at the base to specific details at the pinnacle. In Gorman and Clayton's pyramid, the base has preliminary preparation that forms the foundation on which subsequent stones are laid. The major components of the first stage are: topic choice, problem statement, literature review and theoretical framework. These components are addressed sequentially and recursively and then the researcher can move on to the second stage that involves identifying potential subjects and setting. The next step in the stage is the preliminary data collection as the research begins to take shape. The third stage involves focused activity. The data collection continues as laid down in the broad plan that is constantly amended as more data are collected. As the plan is amended and further data added, the focus of activity becomes more specific. Data collection becomes narrowed to specific topics, themes and ideas within the site or subject. At the pinnacle of the pyramid, with the more focused data gathering, the researcher concentrates data analysis on those aspects judged to be most significant for the project (Gorman and Clayton, 2005, p. 38). In qualitative research, data gathering and methods are intertwined. Hence the methods and data gathering techniques will be discussed together under qualitative research methods.

Qualitative research methods in library and information science

Qualitative LIS researchers use four main methods to collect and analyse their data: observation, interviewing, group discussion and historical study. The specific method that a researcher chooses will be the one that will best answer his research questions. Historical research has been covered in previous sections. A description of the other three methods is given below.

Observation

LeCompte *et al.* (1993) describes observation as a method relying on watching, listening, asking questions and collecting things. Jorgensen (1989) agrees with this definition but notes that it is critical for researchers to keep an open mind. Fraenkel and Wallen (2006) describes it as a method that involves observing people as they go about their daily activities in their natural setting and systematically recording observable phenomena. The degree of observer participation can vary considerably. According to Gold (1969), there are four different positions on a continuum of roles that researchers play when using the observation technique: complete participant, participant-as-observer, observer-as-participant and complete observer. Observation method like any other method has advantages and disadvantages. One advantage of the observation is that it serves as a check, enabling the researcher to verify that individuals are doing what they believe they are doing. The reason is that researchers encounter reports of activities and beliefs that do not match their observed behaviour. Other advantages are that it: permits the study of people who otherwise may be unwilling to give reports of their own activities; permits the study of the people who are unable to give reports of their own activities, such as children and the elderly; allows behaviour to be observed in its natural setting; allows a researcher perspectives or degrees of involvement with the situation or activity being observed;

allows analysis of data in stages as the researcher gained an understanding of its meaning.

Observation method also has some disadvantages. People change their behaviour when they are aware they are being watched. The solution to this is that the researcher should blend into the environment so that they become unnoticeable, but this may also be an ethics issue. Not all types of event lend themselves to observation. Some are too far drawn and some are too brief, yet others are too intimate to observe such as the unconscious decisions users make during online searching. Another disadvantage is the subjectivity of the researcher. This is important in information science when the observer is a professional in the area being observed. Finally, observation can be very time consuming. For a detailed account of qualitative research for information professionals, see Gorman and Clayton (2005).

Interviews

Interviews are a valuable qualitative method that has the advantage of immediacy, mutual exploration, investigation of causation, speed and personal contact (Gorman and Clayton, 2005). Interviews allow the respondent to move back and forth in time and its flexibility allows the researcher to probe, to clarify and to create more questions based on what has been heard. Open-ended questions may lead to unexpected insights. Its disadvantages are: it is costly, uncritical, too personal and open to bias.

Interviews can take up a lot of the researcher's time in execution, recording, transcribing and organizing the results. Secondly, verbal data are susceptible to errors in interpretation. Third, anonymity is lost because interviews are face-to-face and respondents might not be truthful if sensitive or embarrassing questions are asked. Finally, there is a potential danger of bias. For instance, the first impression, approach of the interviewer and demeanour may affect the quality and direction of the interview. Because of these limitations, interview should only be used as one of the methods for data collection. This technique of using a number of approaches for data collection is called triangulation.

Types of interview

There are two main types of interview: structured and unstructured. Structured interviews are those where the interviewer predetermines the question and answer categories. This is called a closed, fixed response (Patton, 2001). The weakness of this approach is that the respondents must fit their experiences into the researcher's categories. However, data analysis is simple and responses can be compared and easily aggregated.

In unstructured interviews, neither the question nor the answer categories have been predetermined. Instead, the researcher relies on the respondents' answers. Often, a researcher may prepare an interview guide through which the research topic is explored in-depth. Patton (2001, pp. 341–345) subdivided unstructured interviews into subtypes: informal conversational interview, interview guide approach and standardized open-ended interview.

1. *The informal conversational interview*. This method relies entirely on the spontaneous generation of questions or the natural flow of an interaction, typically an interview that occurs as part of an ongoing observation. During an informal conversational interview, the persons being interviewed may not even realize they are being interviewed (Patton, 2001). This category is less suited for the inexperienced interviewer.

2. *General interview guide.* This approach involves outlining a set of issues that are to be explored with each respondent before interviewing begins. The issues in the outline need not be taken in any particular order and the actual wording of questions to elicit responses about those issues is not determined in advance. The interview guide simply serves as a basic checklist during the interview to make sure that all relevant topics are covered. The interview guide presumes that there is common information that should be obtained from each person interviewed, but no set of standardized questions are written in advance. The interviewer is thus required to adapt both the wording and the sequence of questions to specific respondents in the context of the actual interview. This entails a framework within which the interviewer will develop questions, sequence those questions and make decisions about which information to pursue in greater depth. One does not have pre-conceived ideas of what to expect (Patton, 2001). This could be a limitation.

3. *Standardized open-ended interview.* This consists of a set of questions that are carefully worded and arranged with the intention of taking each respondent through the same sequence and asking each respondent the same questions with essentially the same words. Flexibility in probing is more or less limited, depending on the nature of the interview and the skills of the interviewers. The standardized open-ended interview is used when it is important to minimize variation in the questions posed to respondents. This reduces the possibility of bias that comes from having different interviews for different people, including the problem of obtaining more comprehensive data from certain persons while getting

less systematic information from others. A standardized open-ended interview may be particularly appropriate when a large number of people are to conduct interviews on the same topic and the researcher wishes to reduce the variation on the responses due to the fact that different interviewers will ask questions on a single topic in different ways. By controlling and standardizing the open-ended interview, the researcher obtains data that are systematic and thorough for each respondent but the process reduces spontaneity (Patton, 2001). Apart from the open-ended interview questions, one can use probe questions or statements, such as: 'What do you mean?' 'I am not sure I am following you.' 'Would you explain that?' 'What did you say then?' 'What were you thinking at the time?' 'Give me an example.' 'Tell me about it.' 'Tell me more.' 'Take me through the experience.' These probe questions help to clarify responses and make the results more useful.

Focus groups

Another type of qualitative data collection is focus groups. The focus group is a group interview designed 'to explore in depth the feelings and beliefs people hold and to learn how these feelings shape overt behavior' (Goldman and MacDonald, 1987). They are called focus groups because the discussion starts out broad and then narrows down to focus on the topic of the research. Focus groups can be used in academic libraries to gather users' perceptions of services and collections. The focus groups method can be used as a stand alone or in conjunction with other qualitative or quantitative methods.

Advantages and disadvantages of focus groups

As Young (1993) indicated, focus groups have several advantages. These include:

- A variety of perspectives and explanations can be gathered from one session.
- They are easy to set up.
- Usually take less time than other methods.
- Responses from others might stimulate people to suggest ideas that might not occur to them on their own.
- Participants use their own words.
- Focus group question design is flexible and can clarify confusing responses.
- In social settings, such as the ones focus groups provide, people are less inhibited than in individual interviews.
- Moderators are able to ask follow up questions.
- Focus groups often detect ideas that can be investigated further.
- Focus groups offer unexpected insights and complete information.
- Focus groups are excellent ways to collect preliminary information.

One disadvantage is that a strong individual can dominate the discussion, leaving little opportunity for others to express their views. Focus groups are susceptible to bias and they could be costly. Information from focus groups may not accurately reflect the attitude of the entire population. The success of focus groups depends on the question skills of the moderator.

Focus groups in an online environment

Online focus groups have the convenience of space and location. No travel required and all geographic limitations are eliminated. Also, sense of anonymity may allow participants to express their opinions honestly and spontaneously. However, online focus groups are only comfortable for computer-literate participants, and it is more difficult for the interviewer to prompt them with probes and follow-up questions. Its success might depend on the computer literacy level of the facilitator as well. In-depth information may not always be available and body language and facial expression, which may provide crucial cues, are absent. Also, emotions conveyed through tone of voice cannot be observed or recorded. Keeping participants on target in an online focus group is challenging. The speed of the conversation and the non-linear nature of the discussion may necessitate more probes and follow-up phrases.

Online discussion can be achieved by the use of software such as 'artafact' (http://www.artafact.com/) and services such as e-Focus groups (http://www.e-focusgroups.com/). For further reading on focus groups see Powell and Connaway (2004), Gorman and Clayton (2005), Young (1993) and Litosseliti (2003).

Conclusions

Research can be categorized into quantitative and qualitative research.

Research design can also be classified into two broad categories, experimental and non-experimental designs. In experimental designs, the treatment variable is manipulated by the researcher. Experimental can be subdivided into true experimental, pre-experimental and quasi-experimental designs. True experimental research utilizes random selection as well as random assignment of research participants. In the non-experimental design, there is no manipulation of the treatment variable. Qualitative methods utilize non-experimental designs. The next thing a researcher must decide after selecting a research problem is the selection of appropriate research design and research methodology. The choice of an appropriate design and method is crucial to a successful research project.

5

Data collection

Once the research problem has been formulated, and an appropriate research design chosen, it becomes evident what type of information will be needed and what type of analysis will be suitable. Information in the form of facts is one of the essential raw materials of research. These facts called data, are the means by which a researcher understands the phenomenon of the world around him. The particular data collection and analysis methods are always determined by the nature of what one wants to find out, the characteristics of the research problem and the specific sources of information. Data fall into various categories; demographic information such as age, gender ethnicity, religion and so on is one kind of data; scores from a commercially available or researcher prepared tests are another. Responses to the researcher's questions in an oral interview or written replies to a survey questionnaire are other kinds. Essays written by students, grade point averages obtained from school records, performance logs kept by coaches, anecdotal records maintained by faculty, teachers or counsellors—all constitute various kinds of data that researchers might want to collect as part of research investigation. An important decision for every researcher to make during the planning phase of an investigation, therefore, is what kind of data he intends to collect. The device (such as a pencil and paper test, print and online questionnaires, or a rating scale) the researcher uses to collect data is called an instrument (McMillan, 2008). The whole process of preparing to collect data is called instrumentation. It involves not only the selection or design of the instruments but also the procedures and the conditions under which the instruments will be administered. Several questions arise:

1. Where will the data be collected? This question refers to the location of the data collection, online, in the library, a laboratory, a private home or the street?

2. When will the data be collected? This question refers to the time of collection, in the morning, afternoon, evening or over a weekend?

3. How often are the data to be collected? This question refers to the frequency of collection, that is, how many times are the data to be collected, only once, twice or more than twice?

4. Who is to collect the data? This question refers to the administration of the instruments, the researcher or someone selected and trained by the researcher?

These questions are important because how researchers answer them may affect the data obtained. It is a mistake to think that researchers need only locate or develop 'good' instruments. The data provided by any instrument may be affected by any or all of the preceding considerations (McMillan, 2008).

Researchers make a distinction between primary and secondary data. This is based on the sources of the data. Primary sources are those from which the researcher can gain data by direct observation or measurement of the phenomenon in the real world undisturbed by any intermediary interpreter. Data from primary sources can be results from surveys administered by the researcher, reports of direct observations of events or conditions or recordings of experiences of participants in the study. Raw data can also be obtained from other sources such as repositories of data collected by government agencies or organizations for research purposes. Examples are the Integrated Postsecondary Education Data System (IPEDS) and the National Center for Educational Statistics (NCES). These are called secondary data because an intermediary has been involved in their collection.

Primary data and secondary data should not be confused with primary sources and secondary sources when considering the literature. Primary sources are those that are published directly from research, such as dissertations, theses, journal articles and conference papers. Secondary sources are those that have been subjected to some interpretation such as writings in books, newspaper reports and other publications. They cannot be viewed as original works, but they are very invaluable in the early stages of research when exploring subjects and seeking problem areas. The types of data needed also depend on the type of research. Qualitative versus quantitative research designs is discussed in Chapter 4.

Population and sampling

Sampling is one of the most crucial steps in research. The first step in gathering data is to identify which population the researcher wishes to study. Population is the total of all cases that conform to a pre-specified criterion or set of criteria. Members of the population must be readily accessible to the researcher. From the population the researcher selects a sample. A sample is a group selected systematically from a larger group in order to make inferences about the larger group. The process of selecting a representative part of a population is called sampling. Sampling is necessary because the population is too big to study and parts of the population may not be accessible. Also, a census obtained inaccurately may provide less reliable information than a carefully obtained sample.

- Samples must be representative of the population, that is, it does not systematically vary in any important way from the population. Random samples should mirror the characteristics found in the population.

- Sample size must be large enough to result in accurate estimation of the population.

Types of sampling methods

1. *Random or probability sampling*:

- *Simple random sampling.* Every element in the population has equal probability of being selected.

- *Stratified (proportional, disproportional).* Samples are drawn randomly from particular categories or strata of the population. You want the sample to be as much like the population as possible. In the stratified sampling method you make sure that each stratum is represented in the same proportion in both the population and sample.

- *Cluster sampling.* This method involves randomly sampling groups rather than individuals from a population.

2. *Non-random or non-probability sampling.* The probability of selection is unknown and it may not provide a representative sample.

- *Convenience sampling.* A group of subjects is selected not because they are representative of a specified population, but merely because they are conveniently available. This sample may be biased.

- *Purposive sampling.* The sample is composed of individuals selected deliberately because they are thought to possess desired information about the population.

- *Systematic sampling.* Samples are obtained by selecting subjects at specific intervals from a list. For example, you may select every 10th subject or case from a list of the total population under study.

Sample size

How big should a sample be? The answer to this question is not an easy one. It depends on several parameters. It depends on the size of the population, the type of research, the type of analyses, whether you want to generalize to the population, and also depends on your time and resources. The general rule of thumb of sample size is 100 subjects or items for descriptive study, 50 for correlational study and 30 per group for experimental, causal and comparative studies.

Sampling bias

This is a tendency to favour the selection of units (people or groups) that have particular characteristics. This can cause an error in sampling. It can be minimized by random sampling and stratified sampling.

Gathering quantitative data

Quantitative online data collection instruments

The type of research dictates what and how data will be collected. In quantitative research, surveys are popular means for data collection. The technology for online survey research is young and evolving. Until the twenty-first century, creating and conducting an online survey was a time-consuming task that required knowledge of web authoring programs, HTML code and scripting programs. Today, survey authoring software packages abound commercially and as free open source packages. This makes online survey research much easier and faster. One of the most frequently used software for online collection of data is *Survey Monkey* (http://www .surveymonkey.com). It enables anyone to create professional online surveys quickly and easily. Survey Monkey lists 10 reasons why researchers should use it. It is affordable, easy to use, flexible, intuitive, secure and limitless, has respect for privacy and is powerful—it has the skip logic feature and other advanced validation and total customization, it has the capability for encryption with additional charges and is customer oriented. It works well for pilot projects, teaching, simple jobs and it is great if you have little institutional IT support.

Survey Monkey also has its limitations. The researcher does not have control of his participants because the data reside on the Survey Monkey server. Secondly, the survey is linear in nature, once there is a response, they close it and you can never make changes to it anymore. The only way one can make corrections is to export it, clean it and send it out again. But the most profound criticism is the security issue. Because the researcher does not have complete control of the data, there may be security and privacy problems for Institutional Review Board approval.

Another open source web survey and form creation tool is NSurvey, an advanced survey and form application that will provide you with professional features such as matrix questions, multi-language surveys, branching, data export, report builder and active directory support. NSurvey is flexible and extensible (through plug-ins) whose form engine and user friendly editor will help you create any survey or form in just a few minutes. More information can be obtained from the NSurvey web site at: http://www.nsurvey.org/. NSurvey has some limitations like most other survey packages. It is branded with its logo and only has a maximum of two simultaneous Web connections.

LimeSurvey

The third open source web survey software is LimeSurvey formerly called PHP surveyor.

This is very similar to NSurvey. LimeSurvey lists over 23 different features on the website. However, one of its greatest strengths is that it supports over 30 different languages. More information can be obtained from: http://www.limesurvey.org/content/view/13/80/lang,en/.

Whatever method you use, collection of data is one of the most crucial elements of research. Bad data will result in an inaccurate result that ultimately is the product of bad research. Data can be collected in a number of ways. One method for gathering quantitative data is through questionnaires. Surveys are the most popular instruments because of their versatility. They could be administered in print with paper and pencil or electronically through the Web.

Survey design

Designing a simple questionnaire for administration to a sample of respondents requires many decisions about the items to be asked, the wording and ordering of the questions (Manski and Molinari, 2008, p. 264). Online survey designs follow the same principles and are not much different from paper surveys. Let us start by looking at paper surveys. Good surveys using the Tailored Design Method (TDM) (Dillman, 2007) demonstrate the ability to achieve a high response rate. The method exhibits a series of four carefully timed mailings, personalized by typing individual names and addresses above preprinted letters. Its distinguishing feature is that rather than relying on one basic procedure for all survey situations, it builds effective social exchange through knowledge of the population to be surveyed, respondent burden and sponsorship. Its goal is to reduce overall survey error, with particular emphasis on non-response and measurement. The most important concept underlying TDM has to do with applying social exchange ideas to understanding why respondents do or do not respond to questionnaires (Dillman, 2007). According to Dillman (1991), in the 20 years since its development, the TDM has been used for thousands of surveys and when used in its entirety, the method has consistently produced higher response rates than are traditionally expected from mail surveys.

Much has changed, however, since 1978 when the TDM was first used. Information explosion and population growth have resulted in large sample sizes. The huge amount of mailings makes personalization almost impossible. Also, using the same protocol for all mailings is a great shortcoming. Traditional postal mailing is not the only way of sending and retrieving a self-administered questionnaire. In the digital age, electronic mail, the World Wide Web, and interactive voice response to taped telephone messages make possible the delivery and retrieval of questionnaires electronically.

Constructing a questionnaire

People do interpret concepts in different ways and words mean different things to different people. The goal of writing effective survey questions for self-administration is to develop a query that respondents will interpret in the same way. This is a difficult thing to do. There are many competing concerns. Ambiguity, use of jargon, unnecessary information, and long-winded sentences are some of the shortcomings of a poorly designed questionnaire. A questionnaire is the researcher's attempt to capture the distribution of an attitude, belief, behaviour or attribute of each respondent in a survey population. Therefore, in order for an inquiry to constitute a survey question, it must require an answer. For example, see box below.

If you searched the catalogue yesterday, did you get a good response rate?

> Yes
>
> No

A respondent who did not search the catalogue yesterday could not answer this question.

When you search Pubmed which wildcard do you use?

> *
>
> #
>
> @
>
> Other

A respondent who does not search PubMed could not answer this question because the question does not apply.

Questions on a questionnaire

The use of introductory phrases, such as 'If' or 'When', means some respondents are not required to answer. In that case, it is difficult to distinguish non-response from those to whom the question does not apply. All respondents must be given the opportunity to answer every question they are asked.

Another attribute of a poorly designed questionnaire is the inclusion of questions that require judgement, for instance—you are more likely to get better results with Pubmed than with Pubmed Central:

- agree
- strongly agree
- somewhat agree
- strongly disagree.

This depends on the opinion of the respondents and the answer may be inconsistent with different respondents. In order to have an effective questionnaire, it is important to understand whether creating an answer demands considerable thought or calculation on the part of the respondents.

How old will your daughter be in 2020?

    = 20

    = 25

    = 35

Response categories sometimes mean more than just words to respondents. For instance:

How often do you study in the library?

Less than 5 hours a week

    = 1–2

    = 3–4

    = 4–4.45

More than 5 hours a week

    = 5.5–6

    = 6–7

    = 7–8

Respondents who do not have an obvious answer may respond to this question partly in terms of where they see themselves in relationship to other students. Beware of vague response categories.

Some information is off limits for some respondents. For instance, respondents may be unwilling to reveal information about events in their past that are not complimentary such as record of petty thefts or drug use. In self-administered surveys, these should be avoided as much as possible. Otherwise, non-response rate or missing values will be high. Researchers sometimes design survey questions without consideration for the motivational factors in self-administered questionnaires. For instance, it may be required that the respondent consult another instruction or code book to understand an unclear question or the questions may be in a matrix format that are arranged in rows and columns. Unless, these are administered by an interviewer, it is likely that the respondents skip those questions giving rise to missing values.

Some researchers collect information in more than one mode, which means data collected in one should be comparable with the other. Several mode differences occur in self-administered and interview surveys. In view of the digital age and the introduction of electronic survey technologies, these are challenges. However, questions can be reworded to neutralize the effects of mode. One survey structure that is commonly used is skip sequencing.

Skip logic

Skip sequencing is a widespread survey practice in which the response to an opening question is used to determine whether a respondent should be asked certain subsequent questions (Manski and Molinari, 2008, p. 264). The goal is to eliminate inapplicable questions.

Example: The use and non-use of E-print archives

1. Do you use E-print archives?

   - Yes
   - No

If yes, which one?

- arxiv math
- arxiv physics
- cogprints
- other.

If you answer No to question 1 go to question 9

Skip sequencing saves survey costs by asking a broad question first and then following up with more specific ones only when the answer to the broad question meets specific criteria.

After writing the questions, you choose an appropriate question structure. There are three ways a survey question can be structured. One way is to post a query as an open-ended question, which means no answer choices are given. The others provide answer choices that can be structured as closed-ended in either of two ways, as ordered or unordered response categories.

Open-ended questions

Open-ended questions in self-administered questionnaires pose a challenge to survey research because of the inability to get adequate answers. The probe questions that usually follow open-ended questions in interviews are missing because there is no interviewer.

Example:

Why do you use E-print archives?

Reasons for using

The answer to this question may not be adequate. It depends on the extent to which the respondent is able to think hard to give adequate and complete answers. Other open-ended questions are not as challenging, for instance,

- What is your current position?
- How long have you been in this position?
- What was your former position?

These questions try to get the respondent's employment history rather than just leaving the first one as open-ended, follow-up questions help to get more information. In short, open-ended questions are often useful in self-administered surveys but the usefulness depends upon the nature of the questions as well as the way in which they are structured.

Closed-ended questions with ordered response categories

This type of question is most useful when one has a well-defined concept for which an evaluative response is wanted. *Example*: 'To what extent do you favour or oppose food and drink in libraries?'

- Strongly favour
- Somewhat favour
- Neither favour nor oppose

- Somewhat oppose
- Strongly oppose.

Scalar concepts that might be used to evaluate a concept idea include:

- Strongly agree to strongly disagree
- Very favourable to very unfavourable
- High priority goal to low priority goal
- A complete success to a complete failure.

A scale of 1–7 is very popular, where 1 means lowest possible quality and 7 means highest possible quality.

Generally, these types of scales request answers the respondents may not have ready-made and may therefore be subject to considerable measurement error. Using closed-ended questions require making decisions as to what type of scale, and what response choices will be most appropriate.

Closed-ended questions with unordered responses

Questions with unordered categories may consist of several concepts that must be evaluated in relation to each other. Generally, closed-ended questions with unordered categories are difficult for respondents to answer because of the amount of information that must be processed. *Example*: 'Which is our most important accomplishment this year?'

- digital projects
- expansion of readers' spaces
- opening graduate reading room
- increase public computer workstations.

Responding to any of these questions requires considerable effort. The first question concerns evaluating against four, then three, then two to come up with the most important accomplishment.

Writing effective survey questions

Writing effective survey questions depends on the right choice of words. Keep it simple. Survey respondents may come from a variety of backgrounds so use simple words, but not at the expense of appropriateness of level. Start by trying to find synonyms that are likely to be understood by more people. You should be careful so as not to appear to be talking down to your respondents instead of communicating with them. Avoid specialized words or jargons, for example, use car instead of automobile. While keeping it simple be aware of the length of your sentences. Keep questions as short as possible. In long-winded sentences undue emphasis could be placed on unimportant words and important words get missed. Use complete sentences to ask questions while avoiding vague quantifiers when a more precise estimate can be obtained. For example: 'How often do you re-shelve books in a 24-hour period?'

- never
- rarely
- occasionally.

This could be revised to read:

- not at all
- six times
- four times
- two times.

Avoid making respondents make unnecessary calculations.

Question: 'What percentage of your staff is minority?' A better option would be: 'How many of your staff are minority?' For more information on writing effective survey questions, see Dillman (2007).

In constructing questionnaires there are common types of errors that should be taken into consideration.

1. *Researcher bias*: this is when the researcher unconsciously develops the questionnaire in a manner that will increase the likelihood of obtaining the desired results.

2. *Sponsorship bias*: this occurs when the researcher unconsciously attempts to produce results that will please the funding agency, particularly when the funding body has vested interest.

3. *Imperfection of the design* of the questionnaire may result in biased or inaccurate results.

4. *Time lapse*: answers to the same question may vary over time. It should be realized that perceptions and attitudes are not static.

5. *Circumstances* such as mood of the respondents, ambiguous questions and resistance to the questionnaire can result in biased results.

6. *Response bias*: error may occur when the response rate is so low that the responding sample is less representative than originally conceived. Using TDM as described earlier will minimize response bias.

Online communities in research

Online survey techniques allow researchers to draw responses from all over the world, and from difficult to reach populations resulting in a much larger sample size. Another advantage of virtual communities as sites for research is that they offer a mechanism through which a researcher can gain access to people who share specific interests, attitudes, beliefs and values regarding an issue, problem or activity. For example, researchers can find a concentrated number of older individuals who use computers on the Internet-based community SeniorNet (Furlong, 1989; Wright, 2000a,b). In this digital age the popularity of the Internet increases as more segments of society are using the Internet for communication and information (Fox *et al.*, 2001; Nie *et al.*, 2002).

Advantages of online data collection: Internet survey

The greatest strengths of Internet survey data collection are the potential to collect a large amount of data in a relatively short amount of time, and the elimination of the necessity for the researchers to manually input or process the data. The data collection can continue while the researchers work on other projects (Andrews *et al.*, 2003). After creating the online questionnaire and recruiting subjects, a researcher's primary data collection efforts are complete. Hundreds of respondents can fill out the survey within a matter of days, despite possibly being separated by geographic distances (Bachman and Elfrink, 1996; Garton *et al.*, 1999; Taylor, 2000; Yun and Trumbo, 2000). All responses can be automatically entered into a database such as Microsoft Access. Data from web-based questionnaires can also be automatically validated; for example, if a data value is entered in an incorrect format, or outside the defined parameter, the web-based program can return an error message requesting the respondent to enter the data correctly and resubmit the questionnaire. If such validation capabilities are used, the researcher's concerns about missing or out-of-range responses will be limited. This automatic validation, however, cannot guarantee the veracity of the respondents' answers.

In addition to its efficiency, web-based data collection can be remarkably flexible, allowing randomization of question order and complicated skip patterns. Online data collection also reduces cost of research by eliminating cost of mailing traditional paper surveys and cost of data entry.

Disadvantages of online surveys

Online surveys offer many advantages over traditional surveys; however, there are also some disadvantages and limitations of the online environment. One does not know the characteristics of the research participants apart from basic demographic information, which may also be questionable (Dillman, 2007).

Challenges of Internet data collection fall into three interrelated categories.

1. Challenges of collecting data using new technology.

2. Validity concerns.

3. Ethical considerations.

For data collection to be successfully done:

- There is need of extensive client-server computing and related technological issues.

- There is need for hardware and software.

- The researcher must have expertise in using the web survey packages.

The Internet provides opportunities for unsolicited responses. For example, if a recruiting e-mail is sent to potential participants, this could be forwarded to other individuals not on the researcher's list. When a URL of a web survey is published online, this attracts unwanted participants. The solution to this is access control and authentication. Access control refers to methods for controlling use of computer resources stored on a server. Authentication refers to the identification or the identity of a particular user. Access control and authentication prevent unwanted research participants from gaining access to or submitting research materials. Multiple responding from the same individual could also contaminate the study. Preventing this might be difficult but some steps could be taken to combat the problem.

First, the researcher must avoid extensive cross-postings of research announcements. Second, instructions must be explicit, outlining the need for one and only one response to the research request. Third, the web site must be designed so that respondents receive a confirmation query and once the survey is submitted, the server sends an acknowledgement that the data have been received. Fifth, the authentication method used can issue each respondent a unique identifier such as a code. Once the data are received, multiple responses and unwanted responses can be weeded out. External technical problems can arise from the Internet service provided or the respondents may lack the ability to use the new technology or the willingness to participate in online computer surveys. Reaching the target population through online methods also poses certain difficulties. E-mail messages announcing surveys are frequently regarded as junk and may be deleted from the mailbox or automatically diverted into the trash by screening programmers (Lefever *et al.*, 2007).

Validity concerns

The researcher has no control over what happens in the respondents' environment that could influence the respondent in answering the questions in a certain way. Uncontrolled response environments may influence the participant to respond in a different context from what is being tested. Demographic distribution could present generalizability concerns. For example, the researcher may have a pocket of low-income individuals in the sample that do not have access to computers. Other problems could be environmental distractions, software and hardware incompatibilities.

Designing Internet surveys

The main goal of writing a survey question for self-administration is to develop a query that all potential respondents will interpret in the same way (Dillman, 2007). In addition, the choice of surveying by mail, web or telephone could influence respondents' answers. Survey questions fail for many reasons ranging from the use of wrong words or an inappropriate structure to being not answerable. The following questions could help diagnose problems (Dillman, 2007):

1. Does the question require an answer?
2. Can respondents accurately recall and report past behaviours?
3. Will the respondents be motivated to answer each question?
4. To what extent do the respondents have an accurate ready-made answer to the question? For example, what is the weight of your mother? The respondents may not know this.
5. Are the respondent's response categories likely to be influenced by more than just words?

6. Is the information being collected by more than one mode. Responses to the same questions may be different for the different modes.

7. Is the respondent ready to reveal the required information?

This is a constantly changing area and researchers must keep up to date with the literature and the technology.

Online data sources

Apart from primary data that the researcher or his designate can collect, there are sources of secondary data online for quantitative research. In June 2005, the Association of College and Research Libraries approved *Guidelines for University Library Services to Undergraduate Students*. These guidelines follow the approval in June 2004, of *Standards for Libraries in Higher Education*. Both documents provide approaches to assessing the academic library based on input and output measurements. Both documents urge librarians to use both quantitative and qualitative assessment tools. The NCES now has a mechanism for peer comparisons on various statistical parameters, that is, the NCES Library Statistics Program 'Compare Academic Libraries' tool.

The Academic Libraries Survey (ALS) produces descriptive statistics on about 3700 academic libraries in the 50 states, the District of Columbia, and the outlying areas of the USA. NCES surveyed academic libraries on a 3-year cycle between 1966 and 1988. Between 1988 and 1998, the ALS was a component of the Integrated Postsecondary Education Data System (IPEDS) and was collected on a 2-year cycle. Beginning with FY 2000, the ALS is no longer a component of IPEDS, but remains on a 2-year cycle.

The survey collects data on the libraries in the entire universe of accredited degree-granting institutions of higher education and on the libraries in non-accredited institutions with a programme of 4 years or more. The survey database includes a universe file. The ALS has established a working group composed of representatives of the academic library community to help in co-ordinating the ALS at the state level. The data are valuable research materials to various stakeholders, from Congress to Federal funding agencies, to state and college administrators, but above all to library associations and researchers who use the survey results to determine the status of academic library operations and the profession.

Data gathering for a qualitative study

Data gathering for a qualitative study is an ongoing process. Qualitative data collection involves more than just collecting discrete units of information. Instead, the researcher engages in reiterative, cyclical movement between data gathering and data analysis (Powell and Connaway, 2004). The kinds of data collected in qualitative research includes interview transcripts, field notes, photographs, audio recordings, videotapes, diaries, personal comments, memos official records and anything that can convey the actual words or actions of the study subjects. Methods of qualitative data gathering include: observation and interviews, and group discussion.

Online focus groups

Another method of qualitative data collection is through focus groups, which could be achieved in one of two ways: face to face meeting with participants and through online focus groups that have the convenience of space and location. No travel required and all geographic limitations are eliminated. Also, a sense of anonymity may allow participants to express their opinions honestly and spontaneously. However, online focus groups are only comfortable for computer literate participants, and it is more difficult for the interviewer to prompt them with probes and follow-up questions. Its success might depend on the computer literacy level of the facilitator as well. In-depth information may not always be available and body language and facial expression that may provide crucial cues are absent. Also, emotions conveyed through tone of voice cannot be observed or recorded. Keeping participants on target in an online focus group is challenging. The speed of the conversation and the non-linear nature of the discussion may necessitate more probes and follow-up phrases.

The success of a focus group depends largely upon the facilitator. A focus group facilitator should possess a number of qualities: empathy, experience with group dynamics, the ability to communicate, and the expertise to direct or facilitate rather than control the discussion. The facilitator should be selected based on attributes necessary for conducting the online focus group. In an online focus group, the facilitator should possess a skill set that includes technological and language expertise that will compensate for the lack of the physical cues present in the face-to-face mode. This includes knowledge of the most appropriate software for the situation. Online focus group software allows private communication between the researcher and the facilitator in a separate window during the session. Thus the researcher can guide the facilitator during the actual focus group discussion.

Recruiting for online data sample

One limitation of data collection in the online environment is the non-random nature. In quantitative research where a probability sampling is crucial, this could be a problem. One way to recruit participants is to link to a homepage and ask for volunteers. Giving incentives such as an online vendor gift certificate might draw more people to fill out the questionnaire (Lefever *et al.*, 2007). The reliability of such surveys is in jeopardy. You should understand that online data collection is based on volunteer sampling rather than on probability sampling (Lefever *et al.*, 2007). Likewise for qualitative research, recruiting is one of the most difficult and time-consuming activities of arranging a focus group discussion. The potential participants should represent the target group while being diverse enough to offer a range of ideas. If universal representation is required, online focus groups may not be appropriate as it automatically excludes those that are technologically challenged.

Conclusions

Data gathering is a crucial step in the research process. The most common method for gathering quantitative data is through surveys. In designing surveys, the TDM minimizes the non-response rate. In writing effective survey questions, certain things have to be taken into account. The questions must be written in such a way that the meaning will be the same to the respondents. Online data gathering is essentially the same with the exception that the administration is done online. Online data gathering has some advantages and disadvantages; however, in the digital age, it is the preferred method. Gathering responses could be subject to a number of biases such as researcher bias, sponsors' bias, response bias, error due to circumstances and time lapse. The researcher must take this into account when administering the survey.

6

Data analysis

In research, we collect data in order to find out whether certain predictions we make are true or not. Data analysis is the process of looking at and summarizing the data with the intent to extract useful information and draw conclusions. This is an important step in the research process, without which there will be no results and no pronouncements on whether the hypotheses could be accepted or rejected. This chapter discusses descriptive, predictive as well as inferential data analysis. As seen in Chapter 4, research is divided into two distinct types, quantitative and qualitative. Data analysis in these two types is fundamentally different.

Quantitative data analysis

As this book is mainly for the novice researcher, its treatment of data analysis is neither comprehensive nor detailed. However, it covers the main topics of statistical analyses and a bibliography is provided for further reading. Wherever possible, examples from the literature are given to illustrate the concepts. In this section, a brief description of each type of quantitative analysis is given followed by examples and a list of pertinent resources.

Statistical significance

Before any quantitative analysis is done, the researcher has to set the significance level, that is, the probability level that his result is not due to chance that he can accept. Fisher (1991) suggested that only when we are 95% certain that a result is genuine (i.e. not due to chance) should we accept it as being true. In other words, if something has only 5% probability that it happens by chance, then we can accept it as true and deem it statistically significant. This is the most common alpha level or P-value and it is written as $P<0.05$. However, you can set your P-value at <0.01 if you so desired.

Quantitative data analysis could be as simple as calculating the mean and looking at the distribution of the data around the mean or it can be a complicated series of regression analysis that predicts the relationship of one variable on another.

Software

There is a variety of quantitative data analysis software. Some are as simple as the Excel spreadsheet, some very sophisticated. Choosing the appropriate software is essential. Statistical software package should be chosen in accordance to the type of information being sought. One of the most widely used for statistical analysis in social sciences and appropriate for library and information science is SPSS (Statistical Package for the Social Sciences), now in its 17th version. Types of analysis that could be done with SPSS include:

- *Descriptive statistics*. Frequencies, descriptives. Mean and standard deviation (SD).

- *Inferential statistics*. Bivariate statistics. In this group are: mean, t-test, ANOVA (analysis of variance), correlation.

- *Predictive statistics*. Regression analysis—linear regression, logistic regression.

All these are parametric tests. Non-parametric tests will be discussed later on in this chapter.

SPSS in statistical analysis

SPSS can read and write data from ASCII text files (including hierarchical files), other statistical packages, spreadsheets and databases. SPSS can also read and write to external relational database tables via Open Database Connectivity (ODBC) and Structured Query language (SQL). SPSS output file with extension *spo can only be read by SPPS, but it can be exported to text or into Microsoft Word. As an alternative, SPSS output can be captured as data, as text, tab delimited text, as HTML, XML, SPSS data set or a variety of graphic image formats (JPEG, PNG, BMP and EMF).

SPSS is not intuitive and you should seek appropriate training. It is a proprietary software and a license is necessary to have access. Most institutions have SPSS site licenses and with this license SPSS provides online tutorial and other documentation. Your institution may offer free SPSS training and support or you may obtain training information on the SPSS website at: http://www.spss.com/. There are other resources as well. The helpful ones are: Morgan (2004); Field (2005); Leech *et al.* (2005); and Pallant (2007).

Descriptive statistics

Analysis begins with the examination of the data to determine general trends in the data and clean up any unconventional data such as missing values. To comprehend the research process without misconception, one must understand some research terminology. A brief glossary of terms is given at the end of the book.

Mean (average), median, mode

The first term, the mean (*mu*) also called the average number, is very familiar to most people. In a set of numbers, average is typical of the set. It is the statistical mean. For instance, in a set of numbers 12, 15, 17, 22 and 25, to find the average, we add up the number and divide by the sum of the total number of items in the set. Hence (12+15+17+22+25)/5 = Average = 18.2.

Median

The median is the middle value in the set when the set is ordered in ascending order. In an odd set, the median is the middle number. In an even set, the median is the average of the two median numbers. For instance, the median for the set of numbers above is 17.

Mode

This represents a number that occurs most frequently in a set of numbers. For instance, in a data set consisting of the following numbers: 3, 4, 7, 3, 6, 8, 9, 3, 9, 7, and then 3 is the mode because it occurs three times and no other number occurs that many times.

Analysis usually starts with a close look at the characteristics of the data. This is done by running descriptive statistics, i.e. mean and SD. In examining the data you may find those scores that are very different from the others. These are called outliers and sometimes may need to be removed so that they do not bias the results. The next thing to do is to examine descriptive statistics to see the mean and SD.

Standard deviation

SD is a measure of the dispersion of a collection of values. It represents the typical distance from any point in the data set to the centre. Table 6.1 shows descriptive statistics (mean and SD) for a data set; total population 51. If we are interested in the relationship between two variables, then we should explore the data to see whether as one deviates from the mean, the other deviates in the same or opposite way.

An example of the use of descriptive statistics is seen in Whitmire (2001).

The purpose of the study was to answer two key research questions:

- What factors influence undergraduate academic library use?
- Do the factors influencing undergraduate academic library use change during college?

Analyses

The author calculated the mean and SD of all the variables in the study and revealed that throughout the 3 years of the study, undergraduates engaged in library experiences only occasionally. The mean of the academic library experiences variable though increased each year from 2.07 to 2.10 to 2.14, never rose to 'undergraduates engaging in library activities often or very often' (Whitmire, 2001).

Table 6.1 Descriptive statistics for a data set

Variable	n	Mean	Standard deviation
Graduation rate	232	49.08	15.7
Percentage part-time	232	18.8	11.78

A study by Applegate (2007), charted the distribution of librarians among large, medium and small institutions. Included in the study were institutions classified in the Carnegie classification, 2000 as:

- Doctoral—extensive
- Doctoral—intensive
- Masters I
- Masters II
- Baccalaureate.

In all these categories, the ratios of instructional employees to librarians for public and private institutions were compared. Other comparisons made were the ratio of full-time equivalent students to librarians by Carnegie classification.

Histograms and scatterplots

In exploring the data, some graphical representations are necessary to verify the distribution of the values in the data set. A histogram is a useful device for exploring the shape of the distribution of the values of a variable. Histograms are used for the screening of outliers and checking normality. A histogram breaks the range of values of a variable into intervals of equal length. For each interval, the number of observations falling in that interval is counted. The histogram is constructed by displaying the midpoints of the intervals on the horizontal axis, and the frequencies on the vertical axis. The height above each midpoint represents the number of observations.

The normal distribution has two parameters, the mean and the SD. The SD is a positive number but as you know, the mean can assume any value. In a normal distribution, the mean, median and mode are equal. Therefore, the graph

Figure 6.1 Histogram of test scores showing normal distribution

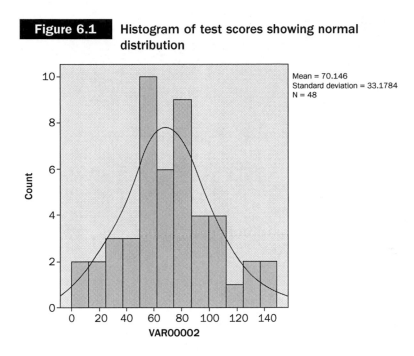

Mean = 70.146
Standard deviation = 33.1784
N = 48

is symmetrical. Normal distribution is important because of the Central Limit Theorem, which tells us that the sums of random variables are approximately distributed if the number of observations is large.

When the data are not normally distributed, they could be skewed to the left or to the right.

Scatterplot

A scatterplot is a plot of the values of one variable against the other. They may suggest a relationship between the two variables or to identify patterns of clusters in the data. Another usefulness of the scatterplot is to detect outliers.

Figure 6.4 is the scatterplot of a data set showing graduation rates and percentage of part-time students. Sixty per cent part time is an outlier as this is not the case with the most of the institutions in the sample.

Figure 6.2 Histogram of interlibrary loan transactions (skewed to the left)

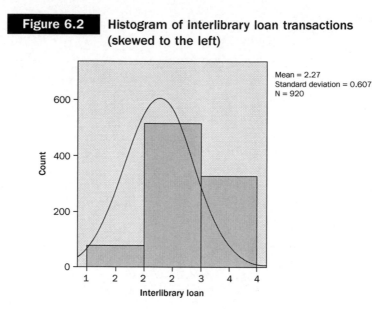

Mean = 2.27
Standard deviation = 0.607
N = 920

Figure 6.3 Histogram of employee previous experience (skewed to the right)

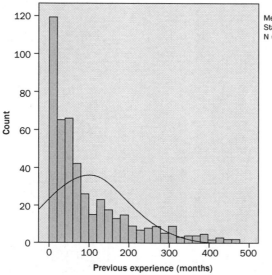

Mean = 95.86
Standard deviation = 104.586
N = 474

Figure 6.4 Scatterplot of graduation rates and percentage part-time

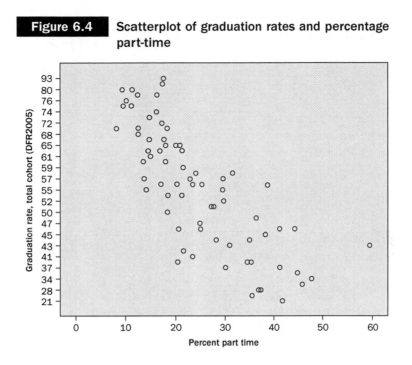

Data analysis

After describing the data, specific statistical techniques are applied in order to get results from which conclusions are drawn. The type of study dictates which statistical technique to use. For instance, for determining the relationships between two variables, correlation analysis may be used. A detailed discussion of correlational analysis is given by Field (2000).

Correlation

Correlation is a quantitative method of research that seeks to find or verify relationships among variables (Fraenkel and Wallen, 2006). In correlational research, researchers seek to determine whether a relationship exists between two or more variables (Fraenkel and Wallen, 2006). The variables could be

Figure 6.5 SPSS command for correlation between gender and starting salary of library and information science graduates

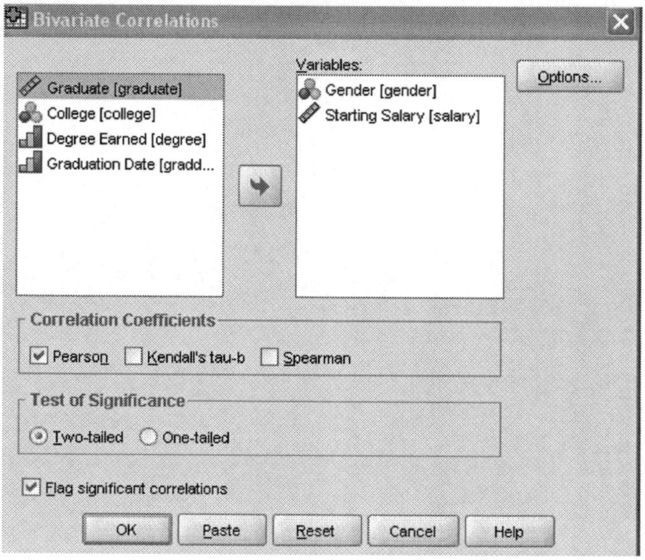

positively related, which would mean as one variable increases, the other increases as well. Or they could be negatively related, which means that as one increases, the other declines. Correlation coefficients range from zero to ±1. The closer the coefficient is to 1 or −1 the stronger the relationship. SPSS command for correlation between two variables (bivariate) is Analyse–Correlate–Bivariate.

Table 6.2 shows the output Pearson correlation $r =0.160$ significant at <0.01.

This means that starting salary is positively correlated to gender. So when gender changes, starting salary changes also, so we know that there is a difference in the salary of men and women.

Correlation is measured by Pearson's correlation coefficient r. Sometimes, Spearman's correlation, denoted by

| Table 6.2 | Correlations |

		Gender	Starting salary
Gender	Pearson correlation	1.00	0.16*
	Significance (two-tailed)		0.00
	n	1,100,000	1100
Starting salary	Pearson correlation	0.160*	1.00
	Significance (two-tailed)	0.00	
	n	1100	1,100,000

*Correlation is significant at the 0.01 level (two-tailed).

rho is used when one or both of the variables consist of ranks. Spearman's correlation coefficient is a non-parametric statistic and so can be used when the data do not meet parametric assumptions such as normality, homoscedasticity and linearity. It can also be used to measure ordinal data. The raw scores are converted to ranks and the differences between the ranks of each observation on the two variables are calculated. The SPSS syntax command is the same as Pearson's correlation but instead of selecting Pearson, Spearman is selected.

t-test

The *t*-test is a parametric test that determines whether or not there is a significant difference between two sample means. The SPSS command for *t*-test is: Analyse–Compare means–Paired-samples *t*-test.

An example of the application of *t*-test to library research is one done by Burkhardt (2007).

At the University of Rhode Island, a three-credit course in the skills and concepts of information literacy was offered. A pre-test was given at the beginning of each semester and a post-test at the end. The pre-test and post-test results were analysed using *t*-test analysis to determine whether the students improved their test scores over the course of the semester; which concepts and skills students mastered and where the course might need revision (Burkhardt, 2007). The author found that on the average, participants performed significantly better on the post-test.

Chi-squared test of independence

Chi-square is a statistical test commonly used to compare observed data with data you expect to obtain according to a specific hypothesis. Librarians often collect data that represent either nominal or ordinal measurement. They then cast the data in the form of a contingency table, where the columns represent categories or one variable, rows portray categories of a second variable, and entries in the cells indicate the frequencies of cases for a particular row–column combination (Hernon, 1994). Chi-squared test of independence tests the association between two categorical variables.

The SPSS command for a chi-square test is: Analyse—Descriptive Statistics—Crosstabs then move one variable into the box marked 'rows' and the other into the box marked 'columns'. Under 'Statistics', check off chi-square. In order to obtain the expected values, under the 'Cells' button, check off 'Expected'.

Example of a chi-square test is seen in Table 6.3 (case processing summary), Table 6.4 (number of people in each group) and Table 6.5. (shows the significance level).

In this example, the researcher wants to find out whether starting salary is associated with gender. The null hypothesis is that gender and salary are independent and the alternative hypothesis is that gender and salary are not independent. Table 6.3 shows the case processing summary, which is a total of the people who are in the study (1100), but Table 6.4 is

Table 6.3 Case processing summary

	Cases					
	Valid		Missing		Total	
	n	%	*n*	%	*n*	%
Gender × starting salary	1100	100%	0	%	1100	100%

Table 6.4 Number of people in each group

			7200	8000	8400	8500	8600	9000	10,000	10,400	10,800	11,000	11,200
Gender	Female	Count	1	1	1	1	0	3	2	0	1	2	1
		Expected count	0.4	0.9	0.9	0.4	0.4	1.3	1.3	0.4	0.4	0.9	0.4
	Male	Count	0	1	1	0	1	0	1	1	0	0	0
		Expected count	0.6	1.1	1.1	0.6	0.6	1.7	1.7	0.6	0.6	1.1	0.6
	Total	Count	1	2	2	1	1	3	3	1	1	2	1
		Expected count	1.0	2.0	2.0	1.0	1.0	3.0	3.0	1.0	1.0	2.0	1.0

the contingency table, it shows how many people in each group.

Table 6.5 shows a statistical significance, *P*-value of 0.000. This means that there is a relationship between gender and starting salary. There is enough evidence to show that the null hypothesis is false. Therefore, the null hypothesis is rejected and alternative hypothesis accepted. Gender and starting salary are not independent.

Table 6.5 Chi-squared tests

	Value	df	Asymptomatic significance (two-sided)
Pearson chi-square	221.68	211	0.29
Likelihood ratio	287.325	211	0.00
Linear-by-linear association	28.227	1	0.00
n of valid cases	1100		

Analysis of variance

ANOVA compares the mean scores of more than two groups. It is generally a form of the *t*-test that is appropriate to use with three or more groups.

Liao et. al. (2007), used ANOVA to study the information-seeking behaviour of international graduate students versus American graduate students.

The study compared library activities of international students with those of their American peers. The means of six library activities of international students were compared using ANOVA. The analysis showed that the international students were much more active than the American respondents in all six activities.

Predictive statistics: regression

Multiple linear regression is the statistical tool most often used to determine the relationship between several independent or predictor variables and a dependent or criterion variable. For example, academic performance of college students can be predicted using such factors as socio-economic background, parents' educational level, high school rank, SAT scores. Given a population of 200 students whose information is known for these criteria, a statistical comparison can be made to predict the performance of an unknown student based on that student's socio-economic background, his parents' level of education, his high school rank or GPA, and his SAT scores.

Example 1

This technique can also be used to study librarians' salary compression as it is described in the following example by Seaman (2007).

Salary compression is the narrowing of the pay differentials between people in the same job but with widely varying years of experience (Seaman, 2007). This is due to a shortage in the supply of qualified personnel. In a job market with more vacancies than candidates, salaries increase at a much faster rate than salaries for filled positions. When resources are directed towards recruiting new personnel, rather than annual merit raises, experienced senior library faculty find themselves earning similar salaries as the new personnel (Seaman, 2007). Librarians' salaries (the dependent variable) can be predicted using such factors as years of experience, administrative responsibility, educational attainment or librarian's rank (the independent variables). If the predicted salary matches the actual salary, then no salary compression is present. If the predicted salary is lower than the actual salary, then salary compression may be present.

Personnel professionals also use multiple regression technique to determine equitable compensation. One can determine a number of factors or dimensions that are believed to contribute to the value of a job such as level of responsibility or number of people to supervise. The analyst then conducts a salary survey among comparable companies in the market recording the salaries and respective characteristics for different positions. This information can be used in a simple multiple regression analysis to build a regression equation:

$$\text{Salary} = 0.5 \times \text{Resp} + 0.8 \times \text{No Super}$$

The regression line is, therefore, determined. A graph of expected (predicted) salaries and actual salaries of the job incumbents in the organization can be constructed. The analyst can then determine which position is underpaid (below the regression line) and which one is overcompensated (above the regression line). In general, multiple regression allows the researcher to ask the question, 'What is the best predictor of ...' Librarians may want to ask which of the multiple social, cognitive and psychological indicators best predict student engagement.

Example 2

The following example shows how multiple regression can be used to find the relationship between a dependent variable and several independent variables.

Allen and Dickie (2007) tested the hypothesis that a positive relationship exists between academic library funding and selected institutional variables believed to be indicators of the demand for library services at the university. These indicators are: enrolment, number of doctoral programmes, doctoral degrees awarded and number of faculty. Eleven years of longitudinal data from 113 members of the Association of Research Libraries were used to create a multiple regression model. Results show that the indicators of the demand for library services are positively related to funding, and most of the associations are statistically significant at the 5% ($P<0.05$) level or less. This means the independent variables have high positive regression coefficients (r). What is interesting is that private universities in the USA spend 21% more than their public counterparts. The presence of a medical school is associated with an 8.6% greater expenditure, and the presence of a law school is associated with a 12.3% greater expenditure. This formula may be useful as a tool for library funding and assessment of adequacy of library budgets, but not a one-size fits all. The authors suggested three applications of the results, application to a specific institution, application to expenditure growth over time and application across libraries.

Logistic regression

Logistic regression is a variant of multiple regression. The procedure assesses the relation between one criterion (dependent variable) and several predictors (independent variables). In logistic regression, the criterion variable is categorical and the predictor variables usually include both categorical and continuous variables. Logistic regression analysis allows the researcher to estimate the odds of an event (one level of the dependent variable) occurring on the basis of the values for the predictor variables.

Non-parametric tests

Non-parametric tests are so-called because the assumptions underlying their use are fewer and weaker than those associated with parametric tests (Siegel and Castellan, 1988). For this reason, they are often used in place of parametric tests when one feels the assumptions of the parametric tests have been too grossly violated, for instance, if the distributions are too severely skewed.

As described earlier in this chapter, non-parametric tests are those that do not rely on the assumptions of parametric tests. An example is given by Antelman (2004). The study's hypothesis is that scholarly articles from disciplines with varying rates of open access adoption have a greater research impact if the articles are freely available online than if they are not. To determine whether a difference in impact exists, the mean citation rates of freely available articles (1), were compared with those that are not (0) for a sample population of journal articles in the four disciplines.

The null hypothesis is that there is no difference between the mean citation rates:

H_0: da = db (where da is freely available, db is not freely available)

Alternative hypothesis is that there is a difference between the mean citation rates:

$$H_1: da \# db$$

Because bibliographic distributions are highly skewed, the author does not make the assumptions that it will be normal. As t-test assumes that distribution is normal, the author cannot use t-test for generating test statistics. Therefore, the non-parametric equivalent, the two-sided Wilcoxon signed rank test was run for each discipline to compare the mean citation rates between open access and not open access articles.

Mean citation rates were given in a table. The percentage difference in means between 1 (open access) and 0 (not open access) is 45 for philosophy, 51 for electrical and electronic engineering, 86 for political science and 91 for mathematics. The SD for Philosophy is 2.51, 2.62; Political science, 2.27, 1.73; Electrical and electronic engineering, 3.14, 2.50; Mathematics 2.84, 1.60. The P-value for philosophy is 0.0092, political science <0.0001, electrical and electronic engineering 0.0006 and mathematics <0.0001. There is a 95% confidence interval for both means.

Though the author did not state the α-level, she concludes that there is a significant difference between open access and non-open access mean citation rates. There is a significant difference in all of the disciplines between open access and non-open access articles.

Qualitative data analysis

The qualitative design method is described in Chapter 4. Qualitative design generates an enormous amount of data.

As such, some analysis must take place during data collection. Analysis involves working with the data, organizing them, breaking them into manageable units, coding them, synthesizing and searching for patterns. Data analysis must not be confused with interpretation. Data interpretation refers to developing ideas about your findings and relating them to the literature and to broader concerns and concepts (Bogdan and Bilken, 2007). Because qualitative researchers collect more information than they ever need, or use, you need to decide on a focus to keep the task manageable.

Analysis and interpretation in the field

Bogdan and Bilken (2007), made some suggestions on how to make analysis and interpretation an ongoing part of data collection.

1. Force yourself to make decisions that narrow the study. In most qualitative research, data collection starts broad, exploring different physical and social space, pursuing different subjects to get a good understanding of the parameters of the setting, issues and subjects researchers may be interested in. After you decide what is of interest to you and what is feasible, then narrow the scope of data collection. For instance, after some initial interviews, you may make decisions such as, 'I want to study the perception of seniors of the effectiveness of online books'. 'I want to interview library administration on their views of library centrality'.

2. Force yourself to make decisions concerning the type of study you want to accomplish.

3. Develop analytic questions.

4. Plan data collection sessions in light of what you find in previous observations.

5. Write many 'observer's comments' about ideas you generate.

6. Write memos to yourself about what you are learning.

Content analysis

The first step in qualitative content analysis is the classification of the data. A classification system is critical; without classification, there will be chaos. More than one person should be involved in the classification. Each person codes the data into a classification scheme separately and then the results of the coding are compared and discussed. Important insights can emerge from the different ways in which two people look at the same set of data, a form of analytical triangulation. Recurring regularities in the data are taken note of. These regularities represent patterns that can be sorted out into categories. Categories could then be judged by two criteria, internal homogeneity and external heterogeneity.

A variety of qualitative data analysis software packages are in the market. A select list is given below:

- NVivo 8 (http://www.qsrinternational.com/). This software removes the manual tasks associated with analysis so that you have more time to explore trends, build and test theories.

- ATLAS.ti (http://www.atlasti.com/index.php). This is one of the earliest in the market. It analyses text, audio, web, graphics and whatever your research material is.

- The Coding Analysis Toolkit (CAT) (http://www.qdap .pitt.edu/). This is Open source software developed by the

Pittsburgh's University Social and Urban Research. It offers a rigorous approach to analysing text.

Examples of qualitative analysis

1. The study was designed to 'identify factors that influence the perceptions of students of colour concerning the library as a welcoming space' (Elteto *et al.*, 2008). They used qualitative methods to study perceptions of students of colour on the issue of library as a place. The goal was to determine if there are qualitative divergent factors along racial lines concerning how students use the library. The authors used two theories to focus on three themes that emerged, Grounded Theory of Symbolic Interactionism and Critical Race Theory.

2. Another example is by Lynch *et al.* (2007) who used interviews as a data collection tool. This qualitative study is a replication of an earlier study done in 1992–1993 to investigate the attitudes of university administrators towards the university library. Data collection was through interviews conducted in 2004 with presidents and provosts of six universities. The interviews were recorded and transcribed, then coded along thematic lines and analysed. The findings were then compared with those of the earlier study. The analysis shows that major changes have occurred in the attitudes of university leaders toward their libraries during the last 15 years. The new findings provide direction for library leaders as they seek out new models of library service and reshape old models to fit the current environment of American higher education (Lynch *et al.*, 2007). This study illustrates a qualitative study as well as replication. Replications of previous studies are legitimate in determining changes in phenomena over time.

Qualitative: observation of user behaviour
Usability testing

Usability testing is an established and accepted practice for evaluating library Web sites, such as OPACS, homepages and portals (Ward and Hiller, 2005). As part of a user-centred design process that engages real users with real tasks, usability testing provides both quantitative and qualitative data (Norlin and Winters, 2002). A number of international standards regarding usability have been formulated in the past, such as ISO 9241-11, ISO/IEC 9126 and ISO/IEC FDIS 9126-1. According to ISO 9241-11, usability is defined as 'the extent to which a product can be used by users to achieve specified goals with effectiveness, efficiency and satisfaction in a specified context of use. The ISO 9241-11 definition is quite broad explaining how to identify information that is necessary to take into account when specifying or evaluating usability in terms of measures of user performance and satisfaction (Bevan, 2001). In a normal usability test, end users complete a set of real tasks while test observers collect information in behaviour, expectations and other empirical data (Norlin and Winters, 2002). During the usability test, a facilitator, ideally a neutral party not directly involved in the design and management of the Web site, will present a list of tasks to a participant. The participant will then try to use the Web site to accomplish each task. As the test progresses, the participant will be asked to speak his or her thoughts and reactions aloud. Approaches to usability testing may vary, but the think aloud protocol described above, where participants use the site while they describe their experience out loud, offers a balance of efficiency and quantity of data gathered (Van den Haak *et al.*, 2004).

Research reports in library and information science journals generally lack the data analysis that allows the formulation of theory for future use as do reports from related disciplines. For example, a usability study of human computer interaction published in *Computers in Human Behavior* included a correlation analysis to classify the relationships between subjects' learning backgrounds and adaptability options regarding the use of computer hardware and software interfaces. Moreover, the authors employed the grey relational model associated with interaction matrixes to analyse subjects' responses via the acceptability inquiry. The correlation analysis helps to identify certain user characteristics in terms of the unemployed middle-aged learners and the grey relational analysis assists in deriving their learning behaviour. This is helpful to improving computer usability for the middle-aged population in the future.

Conclusions

The method of quantitative data analysis used in research depends on the type of inquiry and the type of data collected. Simple descriptive statistics give the trend in the data and graphical representations of the data such as histograms and scatterplots help to identify outliers, non-normality, and non-linearity in the data. Parametric statistics assume that the data are normal, linear, and have homoscedasticity. If these assumptions are violated, then a non-parametric option could be utilized for the analysis. Tests of the assumptions should be conducted before the analysis.

Qualitative data analysis is conducted in the field as the research is going on. At the end of the study, content analysis is done. A variety of software could be used to code and categorize the data along emerging themes.

7

Collaboration

In this digital age, the ability to find and use information effectively is becoming extremely important. Legislatures and institutional administrators are more insistent that schools should be held accountable for students' learning. The library is pivotal in the teaching and learning process of any individual, be it student or not. In today's dynamic higher education environment, the future of the academic library lies in creative and effective collaboration with colleagues across campus. Examining the complex interaction in collaboration, Sonnenwald (1995) introduces the concept of 'contested collaboration' to characterize the communication among team members. Different patterns of work activities, expectations, personal beliefs, specialized language and individual goals may make it difficult for participants to collaborate (Hara *et al.*, 2003).

Definitions of collaboration

Library and information science researchers and practising librarians often talk about collaboration in terms of teams but it is necessary to focus on the real meaning of the word. In many cases, the term is used interchangeably with other terms such as cooperation, partnering, co-ordination and making connections. Bruner *et al.* (1992) argue that the development of clear definitions and operational languages can be critical to research on collaboration. Thus it is important to examine the definitions of collaboration as it is used in research and practice in the past and how it is used today, in the digital world. Collaboration among organizations is infrequent but occurs. Mattessich and Monsey (1992) define collaboration as 'a mutually beneficial and well-defined relationship entered into by two or more organizations to achieve common goals' (p. 7). They described a collaborative relationship as a durable and pervasive one, which aims to accomplish common goals through a jointly structured and shared responsibility. Kagan (1991) defines collaboration through organizational and interorganizational structures where resources, power and authority are shared. People coming together, working to achieve common goals, which could not be accomplished by a single individual or an independent organization? Focusing on collaboration among individuals, Welch (2000) defines it as a dynamic process designed to achieve a shared goal. Schrage (1990) defines it as 'the process of shared creation: two or more individuals with complementary skills interacting to create a shared understanding that none had previously possessed or could have come to on their own' (p. 33). Iivonen and Sonnenwald (2000) also define collaboration as 'human behavior that facilitates the sharing of meaning and completion of activities with respect to a mutually shared goal and which takes place in a particular social, or work, setting' (p. 79).

In reviewing these definitions of collaboration, Hara *et al.* (2003), observed that two common elements emerge: working together for a common goal and sharing of knowledge. However, they noticed as well that working together is not a simple task, nor is the development of a common goal or vision. Sharing meaning, knowledge, resources, responsibility and/or power often involves building social capital and taking risks and trusting others, which can be difficult to do when careers, reputations or other valued assets are at stake (Dirks and Ferrin, 2001; Lin, 2001). In short, collaboration is neither easily achieved nor guaranteed to succeed even though the nature of scientific work requires working together for a common goal and sharing of knowledge (Hara *et al.*, 2003).

The mechanics of collaboration

As Hara *et al.* (2003) mentioned, different patterns of work activities, expectations, personal beliefs, specialized language and individual goals are barriers to sharing one another's specialized knowledge. These differences may cause team members to contest or challenge one another's contributions, although these differences may also enrich collaboration. Unlike cooperation, collaboration is a partnership and each individual brings important elements and expertise to the relationship, so nobody's contribution should be minimized. In collaboration, it is mandatory for the team to develop a common mission (Jehl and Kirst, 1993). It is important to know how collaboration works. Failure to understand how all parties can benefit from working together will result in failure or feelings of exploitation. The management of collaborative effort requires managers, who speak the languages of the various parties and are credible to each of them.

Mattessich and Monsey (1992) named six factors that influence successful collaboration:

1. *The environment.* In the academic environment, tradition plays an important part. Institutions pride themselves on sustaining their long-standing traditions. If collaboration

does not exist in the history of the institution, they are not likely to be confident enough about the process to give their support. However, the changing information environment puts pressure on institutions to change the way business is done.

2. *Membership characteristics*. Members of the collaborative group must share an understanding and respect for each other and their respective organizations. They must be cautious of how they operate their norms and values and be conscious of their limitations and expectations.

   A collaborative group must have an appropriate cross-section of members, for instance, for a project on senior designs, the collaboration should have engineers as well as computer scientists, technicians and librarians on the collaborative group.

   Members of the collaborative group must see the collaboration in their self-interest and must be able to compromise.

3. *Process/structure*. Members share a stake in both process and outcome. It is also important to have clear guidelines. They must be flexible, remaining open to varied ways or organizing and must understand their roles, rights and responsibilities. They must be able to adapt to any changes.

4. *Communication*. Members of a collaborative group need to interact often, share all necessary information, discuss issues freely and update one another as well as people outside the group. This may be through a website, a wiki or a blog. In addition to informal communication, there must be formal communication in the form of publications.

5. *Purpose*. Goals of the collaborative group are attainable within the time frame specified and are clear to all parties. Members of the group have shared vision, existing before

the onset of the relationship or developing during the course of the collaboration.

6. *Resources*. The group needs a skilled convener with organizing and interpersonal skills to carry out his role with fairness. The ultimate factor that influences the success of any collaboration group is funding. Adequate and consistent financial base to support its operations is necessary.

Collaboration comes in different forms. It could be collaboration for reciprocity or for achieving a certain goal.

Teams have an important place in our professional and personal lives. However, not every group is a team and not every team is effective. What is a team then? A team is a group of people with a high degree of interdependence geared toward the achievement of a goal or completion of a task (Parker, 2008). If we think about an analogy for team, we might say that the participants at Richmond, Virginia Ukrop's 10K Monument Avenue run/walk have a common goal or purpose, but they are not a team. They are actually in competition with each other. Teamwork requires interdependence—working together of a group of people with a shared objective.

The following are types of collaboration: research collaboration; publishing collaboration; service collaboration; and instructional collaboration.

Research collaboration

In research, overall effort is a disconnected series of activities operating at many levels on widely differing scales, serving a variety of purposes, and drawing on several loosely connected traditions to do so. The implication of this picture is that there is a lack of coherence in how research is planned. This limits both the quantity and the effectiveness of research. Practitioners such as librarians and information scientists have much to gain from research and much to give, but the disposition of budgets and job responsibilities rarely encourage their active engagement in research.

Greater collaboration and wider engagements are important factors in increasing the effectiveness and influence of research (Morris, 2002). There has never been a better time to collaborate. Networking and advances in telecommunications have made collaboration across institutions, states, countries and, even, continents possible and easy. It is crucial for library and information science researchers to collaborate with faculty. Collaboration starts at the planning stage. The first step in any research process is to determine what to study. The collaborators must begin discussion at this level. After careful selection of a topic an appropriate population to study is chosen. Often times, one needs to collaborate with colleagues from another country, to get the perspectives of a phenomenon or an issue from another culture; for example, a project to survey libraries in the USA and the UK on availability and accessibility of science electronic theses and dissertations, by Subject and Bibliographic Access to Science Materials, a committee of the Science and Technology Section of the ALA (*Subject and Bibliographic Access to Sci-tech Electronic Theses and Dissertations via Digital Institutional Repositories (IRs) and Online Public Access Catalogs (OPACs): Perspectives from US and UK Science Librarians*, 2008).

How can librarians achieve this level of collaboration that results in effective research? Imagine the scenario that follows.

Step 1: application for grants

Many librarians apply for grants from agencies that vary from divisions of the professional body to organizations in the community to federal or state agencies. If granted, this enables them to conduct research projects. The duration of the project could vary from a few months to years. (One important point to note is that where research proposals involve cross-sector collaboration, differing approaches to establishing priorities can lead to delay and misunderstanding. This can be minimized by anticipating such differences before embarking on project design. In addition, if different kinds of knowledge are to be drawn upon in conducting an investigation for instance, knowledge drawn from practice as well as from theory, then people with different knowledge backgrounds will need to work together.)

Step 2: building a team

Collaboration does not just happen. It is essential to build a team comprising of faculty and librarians with a variety of expertise and experience. It is important to understand that collaboration is more than just a gathering of people working together. In teamwork there is interdependence among members and as such, each member must live up to his expectations. Teamwork requires interdependence— working together of a group of people with a shared objective. (A team is a group of people with a high degree of interdependence geared toward the achievement of a goal or completion of a task (Parker, 2008).)

Step 3: assigning tasks

After assembling a team with the necessary expertise and interests, a leader is chosen and tasks are assigned according to the expertise of each team member. Collaboration is successful only when managers can understand the issues of the various parties and are committed to the collective goals.

Step 4: conducting the research

The research project is conducted from start to end.

The full range of expertise needed to tackle research from the original ideas through to impact is located in different professions and different institutions. Collaboration is called for between individuals and between organizations.

Step 5: writing the report

The findings of the research are shared with the rest of the world when they are published. Publishing the report is another kind of collaboration that can result as a co-authored work. In another scenario, a member of the team may provide the technical expertise, which means he may not be a co-author but acknowledged as providing technical assistance.

Useful tips on research collaboration

It is helpful to think through in advance which kinds of people will need to act on the findings and to find ways in which they can be involved at all stages of the research process.

Effective communication tools are needed to facilitate the interaction of the various players at different stages. The full research process calls for a wider range of skills knowledge and understanding than a single individual or even institution can normally be expected to provide. It is important to analyse the roles needed and to plan the way they interact. For inter-organizational and interdisciplinary research, the full range of expertise needed to tackle research from the original ideas through to impact will be located in different professions and different institutions. Specific efforts need to be directed at managing the boundaries between phases, institutions or individuals. To achieve this, the capacity of the system will need to be enhanced as well as that of individuals. Capacity building measures need to be extended to practitioners and policy-makers in their role as potential users of research-based evidence.

Practitioner participation is important in:

- identifying relevant research questions
- advising on sampling or access to research subjects
- contributing knowledge based on practice
- interpreting emerging findings
- elaborating implications of the findings for policy or practice.

Example of a hypothetical collaboration

In a hypothetical collaboration such as the one mentioned above, specific efforts need to be directed at managing the boundaries between phases, institutions or individuals. The librarian principal investigator (PI) forms a collaborative group of faculty, librarians and others within or outside the organization with a variety of knowledge, skills, abilities and expertise, based on the type of project and the goals. The collaborators work together for the duration of the grant and then publish their findings, make presentations and write a report. With everyone on the team contributing his expertise, the project succeeds and the grant was judiciously expended. Collaboration extends to the publishing stage of the project on which the same team may continue to work or as deem fit bring in others who have exemplary publishing skills.

Publishing collaboration

Collaboration in publishing is very common in the scholarly community. In science for instance, it is not unusual to see multiple authors because one cannot actually divorce the publishing aspect from the research process. Collaboration here works the same way it does in other areas.

Service collaboration

Although instructional collaboration has been studied extensively, opportunities for contributing to student services and other co-curricular programmes remain largely unexplored (Walter and Eodice, 2007). Studies of collaboration in this area have focused on library involvement with programmes that bridge the gap between academic affairs and student affairs, such as writing centres, first-year experience and learning communities. However, there is vast potential for collaboration in other student services such as Residence Life, Greek Life, Multicultural Student Services, Academic Advising and Career Services. Across the country, academic libraries and student services units seem to be stepping out of their traditional places and meeting in a new commons. According to Walter and Eodice (2007) the academic mission associated with information literacy instruction can contribute to student services initiatives that seek to address persistence of the 'whole student'. The 'commons' where both student services and academic services, collaborate help to foster student involvement that some scholars have identified as promoting student engagement.

Instructional collaboration

The most common collaborative effort librarians engage in is the one that involves instruction. Instructional collaboration with members of the classroom faculty has been a subject of study for over a decade (Haynes, 1996;

Raspa and Ward, 2000; Bruce, 2001; Dewey, 2001; Curzon, 2004). Apart from helping students develop information literacy skills, they have the opportunity to partner with a teaching faculty for research purposes. However, collaboration among professionals is equally worthy. The potential for instructional collaboration, in particular, has grown over the past decade with the ongoing 'transition in library instruction from a tool-based approach to a problem-solving and learning approach' (Hook, 2005, p. 28). In helping to create an information literate population, librarians need to work with other people or organizations that have the same goal. When the current lack of information literacy skills is combined with the paucity of higher cognitive skills often displayed in student writing, the critical need for collaboration between librarians and discipline faculty becomes clear. The situation calls for integration of information literacy instruction into the curriculum.

Tools

Web

Berners-Lee (1999) described his original vision of the Web as helping people to communicate by sharing their knowledge in a pool, putting ideas in and drawing on the ideas in there. Until now, the Web has achieved this only in part. However, in the event of rapid development in the digital age, there is now social networking software that facilitates collaboration. Klobas and Beesley (2006) describe social software as that which facilitates interaction, collaboration and information exchange, and may even foster communities, based on activities of groups of users. Simply, social software includes any software that brings people together and supports group interaction.

Wikis

Some of the most cited social software are wikis and blogs. Wikis enable many to many communication and they focus on content. It permits more active social interaction. It is used for collaborative research, for instance, building a literature review, storing data, inviting qualitative responses from subjects (Klobas, 2006). The authors of a wiki could collaboratively edit pages of a document to produce one single resource (Klobas, 2006). An example of researchers' wiki is OpenWetWare (http://openwetware.org).

Blogs

Blogs are written by a single author and are based around a timeline. People can comment on a blog posting but only the author can change the posting.

WebOffice

Another tool that could be used for social networking is Webex WebOffice. This is a collaboration suite that uses the power of the Web to make it easy for everyone to work together—from anywhere in the world. WebOffice brings together powerful, professional Web-based business applications specifically designed to make collaboration easy and cost-effective. Everything you need to manage your research on the Web is together in an integrated, centralized place. One can have a 30-day free trial after which one can subscribe for a low fee for as long as the project is on and can cancel at the completion of the project. Another feature of WebEx WebOffice is the Project Collaboration Center. Researchers working on any project can use it as their centre for online collaboration. For instance, two authors working on a paper for publication could use WebOffice Document Manager to store, review or edit the drafts of the paper.

Basecamp

Basecamp is a web-based project management tool. It provides tools tailored to improve communication between people working together on a project. According to the information on their web site (http://www.basecamphq.com/), data are hosted on the Basecamp's web servers so that individuals do not need IT support to mount and manipulate data. This is one of its strengths. Basecamp claims that data are backed up nightly and written to multiple disks. One of the strengths of Basecamp is redundant hardware, so that even if one disk or server fails, nothing will be lost and the system will not go down. It has 99% up time and takes all precautions to keep information safe and secure. Another strength of this software is the hosting; however, this strength may also be its weakness. The data are held hostage and customers may not be able to export them whenever they desire. This is something you may want to think about before signing on to Basecamp.

Voice over IP

Voice over IP (VOIP) such as Skype (http://www.skype.com/). You can download Skype from this address and install it on your computer. You can then talk for free to anyone that has Skype. You can also make video calls if you have a Webcam. Multiple participants can utilize this for meetings, conferences, discussion groups and so on. The beauty of it is that it is all free.

Web conferencing

Web conferencing is the ability to run a Powerpoint-driven meeting on the web.

Hot conference

This (http://www.hotconference.com/) is a proprietary software that is described as one of the most innovative, and reliable conferencing software available on the Internet today. It offers many options; for example, the owner or moderator may enable or disable certain functions to suit individual requirements. When you log in as moderator, you can record the audio from the room in MP3 format. Also included are desktop sharing capabilities and live audio and video. *Hot conference* offers a 1-month full featured trial without any contracts.

iVocalize

iVocalize (https://www.ivocalize.com/) is a Web conference product that enables interactive web conference meetings for today's digital world. It makes online collaboration easier. Features include webcam video, interactive whiteboard, synchronized Web browsing. It is multilingual and it is 100% Internet based with no telephone bridge.

Document sharing

Instacoll (http://www.instacoll.com/)

Today's information economy is built on data—terabytes of data contained in millions of documents that are generated by millions of knowledge workers. The Internet age also mandates that in most cases, these documents have to be shared across multiple people who might not always be in the same physical location. While e-mail was a satisfactory, first-class mechanism to share information across geographical boundaries, its store and forward asynchronous nature pushed people towards looking for real-time alternatives. This is a free software that gives researchers the ability to work on a document with someone else, to be able to edit (Word, Excel, Powerpoint) documents. It provides an easier way to securely share your Microsoft Office documents with remote colleagues in real time. Instacoll is attempting to build a suite of products that bridge the gap between the web and the desktop, creating a new paradigm that merges the best of both worlds. Other products in the suite include InstaAssist and InstaSecure. IntaAssist is a web-based real-time collaboration tool offering customer and sales support. IntstaSecure is a document security software solution that persistently controls access to and usage of electronic information regardless of where it exists without changing the way users work.

VoiceCafe (http://www.worldvoicecafe.com/)

This is also a free software.

File sharing (private)

Shinkuro

Shinkuro software shares files across boundaries securely. Shinkuro's interests and expertise lie in secure Internet capabilities. It works with four operating systems (Windows 98, Windows XP, Linux and Mac OS). Kerr (2004) has this to say about Shinkuro, 'Its best features is its incredibly easy file sharing. You designate a folder on your computer for sharing, and every document that you drag into that folder is shared with your designated Shinkuro group.' Shinkuro offers free backups.

Other features are Instant Messaging and Screen Sharing for a complete collaboration environment.

Challenges of collaboration

Ethical issues

A wrinkle in the online collaborative scenario may be ethical violation because the participants may feel they are being coerced. Ethical issues and how to deal with them are discussed in Chapter 3.

Challenges that occur in partnerships

Challenges exist in every type of collaboration but the biggest challenge is in multidisciplinary collaboration, that is, working with partners from other disciplines. Most common is the challenge of translating an ethnographic approach of research into terms that could be understood by people in business and other quantitative disciplines.

Scenario

One faculty member received a grant to develop a list of best practices for teaching English as a second language. The grant recipient put together a team of eight people to accomplish the task in the specified time frame. The grant recipient was in the school of education of a public urban research institution, but he included librarians, sociologists and high school teachers on his team. His challenge was to explain the details of the project to each member of the team in the language that was comprehensible to all members of the team. Understanding the purposes and objectives of the project they contribute to, have a buy-in in the project. So, this is an opportunity to build relationships across disciplines.

Conclusions

Collaboration permeates all areas of human endeavour. Bringing people with different backgrounds, expertise, knowledge and skills together to work on a specific project enriches the outcome. As we all know, the saying that two heads are better than one is not an overstatement. Engineering and business students are taught early on in their career to collaborate. Library and information science students also engage in team projects. The foundation that is laid during student days can be built upon as practising professionals. Collaborators should take note of barriers to collaboration and make an effort to overcome them.

8

Preparing and publishing research reports

The most systematic and rigorous inquiries in librarianship will have minimal impact if research activities are not reported or reported poorly. Thus reporting is an important facet of the research process. Research reports are detailed and accurate accounts of the conduct of research studies accomplished to solve problems or reveal new knowledge. One of the most important benefits of research is sharing the results with the professional community across the globe in the form of publications. This establishes a presence of that phenomenon in the body of literature, thereby contributing to its growth. This chapter covers guidelines for general writing and also discusses the protocol for preparing research manuscripts for submission according to specific guidelines.

With a well rounded and robust body of literature we can trace the history, issues, trends and outlook of our profession and have a place to share our ideas with colleagues. Apart from this, Gordon (2004) stated 11 reasons why librarians write:

1. Having something to say to their peers

2. Being required to write for tenure or promotion in their academic institutions

3. Wanting to increase the status of their libraries or promote the profession as a whole

4. Wishing to share a technique, idea or programme that has proven successful in their libraries with others

5. Being required by their administration or a granting body to publicize a programme or service

6. Wanting to share the results of professional research activities

7. Desiring to see their names in print

8. Enjoying the writing process itself

9. Wanting to give something back to the profession

10. Being asked to do so by their administration or department heads

11. Wishing to add to their resumes before applying for a new position.

With a full-time job and other commitments, writing becomes a chore rather than an enjoyable activity. Therefore, many researchers fail to present their findings in publishable form. Writing is usually considered a solitary activity, one person in a quiet place typing his ideas on the computer. However, writing could be a social activity. A good writer is constantly thinking about how readers will react to the writing especially for complex professional or technical writing. The readers, in much the same way are engaged in social act, also contemplating what the writer may mean by a piece of writing. If a tree falls in the forest and there is no one there to hear it fall, does it make a sound? The answer is no. There can be no sound without a hearer. Writing is a two-way process. Similarly, readers of in-house documents ranging from training manuals to personal workplans to mission statements, will read between the lines of those documents based on their knowledge (or the lack thereof) of the writer. Their interpretation of a document, as a result, will be based at least to some degree on something other than the words themselves.

Therefore, contexts play a large part in this model of writing. For writers, context shapes—some might argue that it actually causes—the purposes for writing. Moreover, context affects the opportunities, requirements, and limitations and choices writers make as they compose their documents. For readers, context shapes their attempt to construct meaning as they read. Physical context can enhance or diminish their ability to read the document. Social context can affect the extent to which writers and readers share common experiences and expectations about a text. Cultural context will affect the fundamental assumptions, beliefs and aspirations that they bring to the reading of a text.

It might be tempting to consider the elements of this model—purposes, influences, representations of readers and writers, and the various levels of context—as relatively distinct. However, the most effective use of this model of writing as a social activity lies in recognizing that these elements are intimately related with each other. As you consider the part that text plays in the attempts of writers and readers to create shared meaning through text, remember that no single element of the model can stand completely separate from the others.

Writing in Library and Information Science is a form of professional or technical writing that may be equated to scientific writing. As in all scientific communications, the writing must be clear, simple and well ordered. Literary flowery embellishments have no place in scientific writing. A piece of research is not complete until the results have been published and understood. And it will not be understood if writing is not clear and void of jargons. My former teacher once told me that if third graders can understand my material, I would have accomplished my goal. Take note that your publication is not only going to be read by your peers, but also by students just embarking on their careers, scientists reading outside their narrow field and by the ever growing population of non-English speakers.

Types of writing

An application letter for a job, or a resume might be your first piece of writing. A carefully constructed clearly written cover letter, with the reader as the focus may get you that job. On the other hand an inadequate cover letter full of jargons and ambiguity may detract from the message you are trying to convey. Documentation of a process or a training manual, a tutorial or a piece of the strategic plan document is another form of writing. As a practitioner, you may have been involved in any one of these exercises either as a group or on an individual basis. The audience is always the focus, from the new hire, to the members of the department to the senior administrators of the organization.

Publications are not always in print format. In the digital age, they could be websites, online tutorials and online instructions for student employees, podcast of online tutorial such as Web 2.0 or a search strategy. Each of these may be regarded as a publication by some organizations. Because these electronic publications are made publicly available, organizations make sure they go through a thorough scrutiny by peers and superiors. If you have been involved in any of those endeavours, you may have had some practice at publishing electronically.

Publishing for the first time could be a challenge, but approaching it in stages makes the task less daunting. Some organizations encourage their employees to share ideas on a regular basis at departmental meetings or seminars. Presenting research results first at a departmental seminar could serve as an effective strategy to get started. Colleagues can offer feedback that will be useful in improving the study as well as suggestions for a better presentation or writing. Another opportunity to showcase your research finding may be at the meeting of a local chapter of a professional body such as the American Library Association (ALA). These local chapters are small and less intimidating. Information about these chapters can be found on the ALA website (http://www.ala.org/). After your debut at a local meeting, you can confidently take the presentation to a professional conference where the audience is large and more diverse. Presenting at a conference requires adequate preparation and practice, but it does help to consolidate your ideas.

Another way to pre-publish your research is presenting it at a poster session.

A poster session advertises your research. It combines text and graphics to make a visually-pleasing presentation. Typically, a professional poster involves showing your work to diverse groups of people at a conference or professional meeting. A poster session allows viewers to study and restudy your information and discuss it with you one-on-one. This is a testing bed for your findings. Because viewers have time to interact with you one-on-one, their comments and questions may make you think deeper about your work and where it may need improvement. Also, because the viewers are not always known to you, their feedback is more objective and honest. This helps you to shape your ideas before writing for peer-reviewed publication and could make the task less of an uphill battle. Besides, feedback from others could help to improve the quality of the report.

Writing for peer-reviewed publication

What is peer review?

Peer review is the process of subjecting scholarly work to the scrutiny of peers and experts in the same field. The peer review process has disciplinary variation. The processes of knowledge production in the natural sciences and social sciences are similar but the peer review process of the scholarly journals in these disciplines is different. Zuckerman and Merton (1971) noted that physical sciences journals with high acceptance rates tend to use procedures that presuppose that submitted papers should be published and to minimize the chance that worthy papers will be rejected, while the opposite holds for journals with low acceptance rates. These different presuppositions, he says, give rise to different reviewing structures that are distinguished by the number of referees to whom a manuscript is sent. Hargens (1988) constructed two models for the peer review process. In the first model, the editor initially sends the manuscript to one reviewer, if the referee recommends acceptance, the editor accepts it. If the referee recommends rejection, the editor usually seeks the opinion of a second referee to guard against the possibility that an initial referee's opinion is opposed to the manuscript's merit. However, a second negative recommendation is usually an indication for the editor to reject. If the second recommendation is favourable, it means that the manuscript is neither clearly acceptable nor unacceptable. The editor is likely to send a manuscript like this to a third referee whose opinion will decide its fate for that journal.

The second structure employs two initial referees for each manuscript, and requires that both recommend acceptance for immediate acceptance by the editor. If both referees recommend rejection, the editor rejects the paper. A paper that receives a split decision from the initial referees is sent to a third, who determines its fate. Both of Hargens' structures did not assign the journal editor a role beyond selecting referees and compiling their votes. For each manuscript, the reviewers will critic the paper stating its strengths and weaknesses and noting compliance with the standards for reporting on empirical research in the discipline. Standards for Reporting on Empirical Social Science Research in American Educational Research Association (AERA) Publications (AERA, 2006) could be useful to Library and Information Science societies and publishers as well. The standards cover but are not limited to qualitative and quantitative research methods. These standards are beneficial to authors in the preparation of manuscripts that report such work, to editors and reviewers in their considerations of such works for publication and readers in being an informed consumer. After the review, each reviewer sends the manuscript back to the editor with comments and recommendations. The editor makes a decision to:

- unconditionally accept
- accept on condition that the author revises it in certain ways
- reject it but encourage revision and invite resubmission
- to reject outright.

Preparing a research manuscript for publication

In reviewing quantitative research for publication, editors accept well written manuscripts that follow the guidelines and conform to the publishing philosophy of the journal. In the social and behavioural sciences, the *Publication Manual of the American Psychological Association* (5th edn, 2001) is the standard. In order to cover all the bases, you could prepare a checklist for completion of the manuscript. Suggestions for items on the checklist are as follows.

- Choosing a title.

- Abstract.

- Introduction/objective/purpose/hypotheses.

- Review of the literature.

- Conceptual framework of the study.

- Methods.

- Results—results should match the method and research questions.

- Tables and figures—prepare all tables and figures according to the instructions given by the journal. The tables and figures should be self-explanatory, but match the information in the text.

- Conclusions and discussion—in this section, make sure you have answered the questions you started with. If there is need to make some adjustments, you can go back and make them.

- Limitations—do not forget to state the limitations of the study.

- References—use the citation style give by the journal or publisher.

- Appendices.

The following subsections describe what each part contains and the function of each part.

Choosing a title

The title is important as an attraction to potential readers. You want your article or book to be read and cited in other publications. Readers of professional literature in particular regularly skim periodicals looking for interesting articles. If they do not read the actual articles they scan the table of contents. If you have a thought-provoking title, that will attract attention. Articles with dull uninteresting titles are passed up. In writing your title, include carefully selected keywords that identify exactly what you are writing about. Make a list of a few titles and juggle the keywords until there can be no mistake about the message you want to get across. Another reason to have a carefully designed title, is that when the article is indexed, the indexers assign subject headings or keyword descriptors to your article and it is those descriptors that link your title with the subject headings in the indexing database. In the digital age, effective title provides accurate metadata for searching. The title page consists of the following components:

- a running head (appearing on each page) for the publication
- the title of the manuscript
- a by-line or the authors listed in order of their contribution along with institutional affiliation (for each author if different).

The abstract

The first stage in the preparation of a manuscript is writing the abstract of your paper. The abstract is a summary of the content of the paper. It must include a summary of each of the sections contained in the paper. The abstract is by far the most widely read part of the research article. In the electronic age, it is the only part that is read most of the time (Pitkin and Branagan, 1998). In view of its importance, the accuracy of abstracts is critical. A well-prepared author's abstract enables the reader to identify the basic contents of the paper, quickly and accurately and decide whether to go on reading or not. Most journals require that the abstract be not more than 250 words, but you can keep to the guidelines given by the journal of interest to you. The abstract is so important that the review process begins with it and it may sell or sink your paper.

Introduction/objective/purpose/hypotheses

The introduction provides a framework for the problem that is being studied and the context for the statement of the rationale, purpose and objective of the study being reported. The objective or purpose of the study should be clearly stated. Hypotheses, if any, should be clearly worded. A good introduction orients the reader to the importance of the problem by providing sufficient background information. The introduction may also briefly mention the works that have been done in the area being studied, highlighting the important studies. The introduction ends with a statement of purpose, for example, 'the purpose of this study is ...' In addition, statement of hypothesis may also be included, for example, 'the hypothesis is that information literacy influences academic performance.'

Review of the literature

This section gives critical review of the research problem as reported in existing literature. The length depends on the overall restriction on length imposed by the journal and on the extent of relevant literature.

Conceptual framework of the study

The general framework of the study is restated in specific hypotheses and research questions in line with the objectives of the study. Operational definitions of concepts in the research questions or hypotheses are given.

Methods

The methods section describes how the study was conducted. The information should be detailed enough to allow anyone else to replicate the study as it was originally done. For a well-organized methods section the different parts should be subheadings such as: Variables, Instruments, Data/Data gathering, Population/Sample/Sampling and Data analysis.

Here the researcher completes the explanation of how the research problem was addressed. Statistical methods used to test the hypotheses are explained and any other data analysis techniques used are described. The audience level of sophistication in regard to statistical analysis techniques should govern the extent to which technical details of data analysis are explained. This is the most faulted part of the manuscript either because of inappropriate or unsuitable data analysis technique.

Results

This section gives a description of the statistical techniques used to analyse the data and what the results of the analysis were. Results should match the method and research questions. It should be noted whether the results support the null hypothesis or whether it should be rejected. The rule of thumb of presenting the numerical results is that two sets of results could be presented in text form but three or more should be mentioned only briefly in text but well presented in tabular of graphical form.

Tables and figures

If appropriate data are presented in visual formats such as tables, charts, figures and diagrams. According to the APA manual (2001), reporting more than three sets of results should be in tabular form while less than three can be reported in the text.

Conclusions/discussion

In the discussion section, the author is free to explore important relationships between past research, and results of the current study. In this section, make sure you have answered the questions you started with. If there is need to make some adjustments, you can go back and make them. Research objectives may be restated. In presenting the findings, arguments should be made in a logical sequential manner. A report of an evaluation of whether the results meet the researcher's expectations is also given in this section. The researcher has the opportunity to sum up the research findings and what contribution the study makes to the literature. The discussion section is also the place to spell out the implications and limitations of the study as well as suggestions for future research.

References

References comprise the sources that were consulted during the course of the study and the writing of the manuscript. The preferred style is APA 5th edn, unless you are otherwise advised by the journal editor or publisher.

Appendices

An appendix usually contains information that is not essential for understanding the content of the manuscript but important to provide a clear picture of the research process. Usually the appendix will contain the original questionnaires that were used and any accompaniment that explains the questions and responses.

Increasing your chances of acceptance

There are certain things you can do to enhance your chances of acceptance. No one likes to receive letters of rejection from a publisher, yet this happens more often than not. Reasons for rejection could vary from mismatch, quality of research, inappropriate level of audience and quality of the writing. In other words, you have to do your homework thoroughly before sending out your manuscript. For instance, seek out a suitable journal in the area of your research, study the mission goals and philosophy of the journal and study critically the instructions to authors.

Finding a suitable journal

A major factor in the selection of an audience is the chosen communication vehicle. For instance, a research article prepared for a scholarly journal *The Library Quarterly* will be different from the one prepared for a professional journal such as the *Library Journal*. While the former is a scholarly research journal, the latter is a popular journal directed towards practising librarians. Articles in *The Library Quarterly* are based on studies relating to all facets of librarianship many of which are notable dissertations and theses prepared by recipients of higher degrees at library schools. Hence the emphasis, detail and style will be fundamentally different from the ones prepared for the *Library Journal.*

The *Journal of Education for Librarianship*, published by the American Association of Library Schools, reports studies relating to all facets of library education. Apart from research reports, there are countless other forms of writing. One example is description of a process such as establishing an Institutional Repository or planning for remodelling the library building or re-creating user space, or creating an off-site storage. In this kind of writing, you may want to share with your readers, what works and what does not, what you view the best practices to be. Whichever type of writing you choose, it contributes to the body of knowledge of the profession. Finding a suitable journal for every type of writing is a very crucial step as a mismatch could lead to a rejection. The first thing to consider when choosing a journal is the audience. Who does the journal address? This information may be found in the inside cover of the journal or from the journal's website. The mission and vision of the journal will also help in the decision making. Sometimes, the distribution of the journal may be a factor. Is it electronically available? Electronic publications have a wider distribution.

Most journals are now published electronically even when they have a print counterpart. There are several advantages of electronic publications. These include speedy publication and delivery over the Internet, wider and cheaper distribution, alert system, electronic table of contents and linking to full-text articles from the references. You may also want to pick a journal that is indexed by a number of abstracting and indexing services in the field. Another way to avoid rejection is to study the journal's rate of acceptance and rejection. Non-peer-reviewed Open Access journals (OAJ) may be easier target for your initial publication. OAJs charge authors for publishing and are provided free to the public. The idea is to increase authors' visibility and easy access to scholarship thereby promoting their increased impact and usage. The acceptance rate of OAJs may be better than paid journals. The smaller less known journals might provide an opportunity for you to practise your writing before sending it off to the more prestigious ones. Other periodicals that feature Library and Information Science research reports include: *Special Libraries, RQ, Reference Librarian, Catholic Library World, Aslib Proceedings, Information Today, Californian Librarian.*

Rejection

A letter of rejection is a bitter pill to swallow. This is unavoidable sometimes. Some journals receive up to 10 times the number of manuscripts they are able to accept. Your manuscript may have been written well but it may be rejected because the editor does not have a space at that particular time in the issue at hand. According to Caelleigh (personal communication, 2008), space is limited for papers of all kinds. Authors compete for this limited amount of space; therefore, only a small portion of submitted papers is published. If the recommendation of the readers is to resubmit after minor revisions, you may do so or send it to a similar journal. For instance, if you submit a manuscript to *College and Research Libraries* and it is rejected, you may submit it to the *Journal of Academic Librarianship.*

You may have done everything right, but still receive letters of rejection. You must learn to tolerate rejection and learn from it. According to Johnson and Mullen (2007), in order to thrive as a writer, you must become a master in the art of toleration, turning rejection into something positive. The fear of another rejection may cause procrastination and loss of motivation.

Writing

Writing comes from many hours of practice (Ericsson *et al.*, 1993). One common mistake authors make is the use of highly technical language in their writing. Researchers use terms and occasionally jargon that may not be comprehensible to their readers. The same occurs in any field where a specialized language develops to ease the communication among professionals. In writing research reports, jargon should be curtailed to the minimum and, where possible, a glossary of terms should be given to make the reports comprehensible. To test the readability and comprehension of your research, you may gather a group of your co-workers with different backgrounds and present your paper to them the way you have written it. If they understand it, your worldwide readers will too. Listen to comments and incorporate the feedback into the final writing.

Below is an annotated list of potential vehicles for your research reports.

- An example of a journal best suited for process description is *Sconul Focus* (ISSN 1353–0429), formerly *Sconul Newsletter* (http://www.sconul.ac.uk/publications/ newsletter/). It is published by Society of College, National and University Libraries (SCONUL). SCONUL is described as promoting excellence in library services in higher education and national libraries across the UK and Ireland. The articles are concise.

- *College and Research Libraries News* published by the Association of College and Research Libraries is another light reading journal. It accepts articles of a news nature such as grants and acquisitions, professional news about people, preservation news and Internet reviews.

- *Library Resources and Technical Services* (LRTS) ISSN: 0024–2527 (http://www.ala.org/ala/mgrps/divs/alcts/ resources/lrts/index.cfm). Published quarterly, LRTS is an official organ of the Association for Library Collections and Technical Services, a division of the American Library Association. It supports the theoretical, intellectual, practical and scholarly aspects of the profession of collection management and development, acquisitions and cataloguing and classification. It is published both in electronic and print formats. All articles are peer reviewed. Instructions for authors can be found on their Web site: http://www.ala.org/ala/mgrps/divs/alcts/resources/ lrts/index.cfm/. If you do not subscribe to the journal, you can request a sample issue from their Web site.

- *College Research Libraries* (CRL) ISSN: 0010–0870 (http://www.ala.org/ala/mgrps/divs/acrl/index.cfm). An official journal of the Association of College and Research Libraries, a division of the American Library Association is published bimonthly. CRL is a scholarly journal. All articles are peer reviewed. This journal favours empirical research reports. It offers preprints, articles that have been accepted for publication in future issues. So, if you do not subscribe to the journal, these preprints serve as samples of the types of articles the journal publishes.

- *portal: Libraries and the Academy* (http://www.press
  .jhu.edu/journals/portal_libraries_and_the_academy/).
  Published four times a year by Johns Hopkins University
  Press, *portal* presents research findings and covers issues
  in technology on a regular basis. Peer-reviewed articles
  written by librarians for librarians focus on issues that
  affect the practice of librarianship. A core function of this
  journal is to examine the role of libraries in the academy
  and specifically, the libraries' role in meeting institutional
  missions. Information about submission guidelines can be
  found on the Website.

- *International Information and Library Review* (IILR)
  (http://www.elsevier.com/wps/find/journaldescription
  .cws_home/622845/description#description). For international
  perspectives, IILR feature peer reviewed articles from across
  the Globe. The journal focuses on policy and ethical issues
  as well as designing and implementing information
  systems and services in libraries around the world. Both
  print and online versions are published four issues to a
  volume per year.

- *Journal of Academic Librarianship (JAL)* (http://www
  .elsevier.com/wps/find/journaldescription.cws_home/620
  207/description#description). If you are aiming to be an
  academic librarian, take note of this journal. It publishes
  articles that focus on problems and issues that are
  relevant to academic libraries. It provides a forum for
  researchers to publish their findings. It also publishes
  articles that analyse policies, issues and trends.

- *Journal of Library Administration and Management*
  (LA&M). LA&M is the journal of the (http://www.ala
  .org/ala/mgrps/divs/llama/lama.cfm) Library Administration
  and Management Association (LAMA), a division of the

American Library Association (http://www.ala.org/). Information from the journal website says it focuses on assisting library administrators and managers at all levels as they deal with day-to-day challenges. In-depth articles address a wide variety of management issues and highlight examples of successful management methods used in libraries. Common features include interviews with prominent practitioners in libraries and related fields. Others are columns with practical advice on managing libraries. If you are interested in library administration, this journal is a valuable resource. It does not currently have a website.

- *Library Trends* (http://www.press.jhu.edu/journals/library_trends/).

- Apart from the preceding list of journals, *Mortimore-Singh Guide to Publications in Library and Information Studies* (http://www.uncg.edu/lis/PublicationGuide/index.html) provides valuable information for those who want to publish but do not know where to start. This site is hosted by the Department of Library and Information Studies, University of North Carolina at Greensboro. It brings together descriptions and submission guidelines for some of the most prominent English language library and information studies periodicals in print today. It covers over 115 journals.

Some tips on writing

Like doing your taxes, writing may not be your favourite thing to do. You can overcome the barriers of writing by taking some simple steps.

Not enough time

The first barrier to writing that I have experienced and heard from many of my colleagues is time. There is not enough time in the day to squeeze that in. I learned years ago that you can devote a few minutes a day to your writing and still achieve a lot. Some people suggest writing at least 200 words a day (Silvia, 2007). But the most talked about solution to the time barrier is scheduling. According to Silvia (2007), drawing up a schedule and sticking to it is the key to successful writing. Pick a time of day that you are most likely to be free of interruptions. I find early morning between 4 and 6:00am very productive. That way, I get my writing done before going to work. I know it is very hard to keep to schedule in a world full of unknowns, but it has been empirically proven to work.

Writer's block

Sometimes you may lose your rhythm for writing. When this occurs, going for a walk or run, listening to music, doing other mundane activities such as gardening or reading, make your writing juices flow again. Do everything except stop writing. Some prolific writers have suggested that you should change your location, that is, move to a different space. Some writers have found inspiration in their bathtubs or in the showers. For writers with small children, all these suggestions may not work exactly in the same way. Do what you need to do to maintain a relatively stable rhythm. You may even get your rhythm back by watching some educational television with your kids. Getting that rhythm back is important to getting your writing to the finish line.

Conclusions

Reporting is the last major step of the research process. Effective research reports are accurate, logical, understandable, comprehensive and can communicate results to both scholars and practising librarians. A significant and rigorously conducted research can fall through the cracks because of poor reporting. Good reporting can facilitate the replication of studies so that data and results can be verified. Research reports will vary depending on whether it is quantitative or qualitative design. The various steps of the research reports are equally important and deserve careful consideration. Researchers should select an appropriate vehicle in which to publish their reports. Attention should be paid to the instructions to authors of the specific journals to which the manuscript is sent. Rejection should be avoided by all means but where it could not be avoided, it should be managed adequately so that it does not become a deterrent to writing. Skills in writing develop over a period of time with consistent practising. Some tips on improving writing include more writing.

9

Conclusions

Librarianship started in the USA in 1876. Its beginning was signified by the founding of American Library Association, the founding of *The Library Journal* and the publication of *The Public Libraries in the United States of America, their history, condition, and management* (1876), which included recommendations regarding education for librarianship. Training for librarianship was in the form of apprenticeship. Similar developments went on in Europe at this time. This mode of learning was a comfortable concept for librarianship. It evolved into a professional education and continued until the Columbia School of Library Economy was founded by Melvyl Dewey in 1887. However, Dewey was criticized for not requiring graduation from college before entering the programme and for creating an educational programme that was not research oriented. The foundation for library education as we have it today was laid with Williamson's proposal of a 1-year post-baccalaureate programme. Because of the apprentice training, there was controversy about whether librarianship was a profession or a vocation. Library education has gone through several versions of accreditation standards, the latest in 2008.

The curriculum of LIS schools was originally geared towards the practice of librarianship with core courses in cataloguing, acquisitions, collection management, reference and preservation. The need to respond to a rapidly changing technological society prompted the injection of content such as web design, Web 2.0 applications, electronic resources, digitization and networking into the curriculum. Practical training took precedence over theoretical and research oriented curriculum. Early literature of LIS was full of writings about the discontent over the absence of research oriented schools and in some cases attributed the demise of the failed LIS schools to this fact.

The controversy over the curriculum of LIS schools still exists today. Though the word research is used loosely to mean many different things, this book refers to it as a series of steps beginning with identification of research topic, formulating research questions, designing the research, data collection, analysing the data, drawing conclusions and writing the reports. Research methodology did not immediately gain the recognition that other courses enjoyed. Today, it is listed on the curriculum of most schools as a three-credit hour course, which is grossly inadequate to cover both quantitative and qualitative methods. Moreover, it is not required to earn an MLS degree in many LIS schools. Continuing education has come to the rescue of those whose needs were not met by the LIS curriculum, but incentives are not always provided by employing libraries. The Medical Library Association has done a good job of formalizing a continuing education credit granting programme. Without formal education in research methodology, it is left to the individual to seek out courses or programmes that will make him an effective researcher.

In any profession, the importance of research to the advancement of the field's knowledge base cannot be overemphasized. Those who assessed the previous research of librarians have been of a consensus that the quantity and quality have left something to be desired. It is said that library research is non-cumulative, fragmentary, generally weak and relentlessly oriented to immediate practice. Research papers should show evidence of rigour with incorporation of established statistical analysis rather than descriptive analysis of data. If librarianship is viewed as a profession as it should be, then there is need to develop theories by which the profession operates. This can only be done by basic, applied and action research. This is not denying the fact that library-related research is not being conducted. In fact, LIS research has made some progress in terms of rigourousness, sophistication and use of multiple methods of statistical analysis. Both qualitative and quantitative methods have been used to determine relationships and effects of one phenomenon on another. But there is still room for improvement.

It is perhaps not by design that research in LIS is sparse compared with other professions. The conduct of research can be a daunting task, particularly if it is only voluntary. It is hard to add research to the already crowded schedules librarians have every day. Much has to be learned on the regular job, in terms of new technology, new practice or new service that time left for research is limited. Though service is the mainstay of the LIS profession, and rightly so, yet the profession should position itself for continuous growth and engage in active scholarly communication. The curriculum should emphasize an evolving body of knowledge that reflects the findings of basic and applied research from relevant fields. The profession should provide direction for future development and should not lose sight of the need to create knowledge in the midst of the current global information and technological upheaval.

References and additional reading

References

AERA (2006). Standards for reporting on empirical social science research in AERA publications. *Educational Researcher*, 35 (6), 33–40.

Abram, L. and Luther, J. (2004). Born with a chip. *Library Journal*, 8 (1), 34–37.

Allen, F. R. and Dickie, M. (2007). Toward a formula-based model for academic library funding: statistical significance and implications of a model based institutional characteristics. *College & Research Libraries*, 68, 170–81.

American Library Association (2002). *Library and Information Studies and Human Resources Utilization*. Chicago, IL: American Library Association.

American Library Association (2005). *Statement of core competencies. American Library Association Policy 54.1.* Available at: http://www.ala.org/ala/aboutala/governance/policymanual/librarypersonnel.cfm#/. *Policy 54.2.* Available at: http://www.ala.org/ala/aboutala/governance/policymanual/librarypersonnel.cfm#/.

American Psychological Association (APA) (2001). *Publication manual*, 5th ed. Washington DC: APA.

Andrews, D., Nonnecke, D. and Preece, J. (2003). Electronic survey methodology: a case study in reaching hard-to-involve Internet users. *International Journal of Human-Computer Interaction*, 16 (2), 185–210.

Antelman, K. (2004). Do open-access articles have a greater research impact? *College & Research Libraries*, 65, 372–382.

Applegate, R. (2007). Charting academic library staffing: data from national surveys. *College & Research Libraries*, 68, 59–68.

Auld, L. W. S. (1990). Seven imperatives for library education. *Library Journal*, 115 (8), 55–59.

Bachmann, D. and Elfrink, J. (1996). Tracking the progress of e-mail versus snail-mail. *Marketing Research*, 8 (2), 31–35.

Berners-Lee, L. (1999). Transcript of Tim-Berners-Lee talk to the LC's 35th Anniversary celebrations, Cambridge, Massachussetts, 14 April, 1999. Retrieved March 3, 2008 from: http://www.w3.org/1999/04/13-tbl.html/.

Bevan, N. (2001). International standards for HCI and usability. *International Journal of Human Computer Studies*, 55, 533–552.

Bogdan, R. C. and Bilke, S. K. (2007). *Qualitative research for education: an introduction to theories and methods*, 5th ed. Boston, MA: Pearson.

Booth, W. C., Colomb, G. G. and William, J. M. (1995). *The craft of research*. Chicago, IL: University of Chicago Press.

Bruce, C. (2001). Faculty-librarian partnerships on Australian higher education: critical dimensions. *Reference Services Review*, 29 (2), 106–115.

Bruner, C., Kunesh, L. G. and Knuth, R. A. (1992). What does research say about interagency collaboration? Retrieved 20 June 2008 from: http://www.ncrel.org./sdrs/areas/stw_esys/8agcycol.htm/.

Burkhardt, J. M. (2001). Assessing library skills: a first step to information literacy. *portal: Libraries and the Academy*, 7, 25–49.

Busha, C. H. (1981). Library science research: the path to progress. In C. H. Busha (Ed.), *A library science research reader and bibliographic guide* (pp. 1–37). Littleton, CO.: Libraries Unlimited.

Busha, C. H. and Harter, S. P. (1980). *Research methods in librarianship: techniques and interpretation.* New York: Academic Press.

Campbell, D. T., Stanley, J. C. and Gage, N. L. (1963). *Experimental and quasi-experimental designs for research.* Chicago, IL: R. McNally.

Cohen, L. and Manion, L. (2000). *Research methods in education,* 5th ed. London: Routledge.

Conant, R. W. (1980). *The Conant Report: a study of the education for librarian.* Cambridge, MA: MIT Press.

Curzon, S. C. (2004). Developing faculty-librarian partnerships in information literacy. In F. Rockman (Ed.), *Integrating information literacy into higher education curriculum* (pp. 42–60). Chicago, IL: Association of College & Research Libraries.

Dewey, B. I. (Ed.). (2001). *Library user education: powerful learning, powerful partnerships.* Lanham, MD: Scarecrow Press.

Dillman, D. A. (1991). The design and administration of mail surveys. *Annual Review of Sociology,* 17, 225–249.

Dillman, D. A. (2007). *Mail and Internet surveys: the tailored design method,* 2nd ed. Hoboken, NJ: John Wiley.

Dillon, A. and Norris, A. (2005). Crying wolf: an examination and reconsideration of the perception of crisis in LIS education. *Journal of Education for Library and Information Science,* 46, 280–298.

Dirks, K. T. and Ferrin, D. L. (2001). The role of trust in organizational settings. *Organization Science,* 12, 450–467.

Elteto, S., Jackson, R. M. and Lin, A. A. (2008). Is the library a welcoming space? An urban academic library and diverse student experiences. *portal: Libraries and the Academy*, 8, 325–37.

Ennis, P. H. (1967). Commitment to research. *Wilson Library Bulletin*, 41 (May), 899–901.

Ericsson, K. A. and Simon, H. A. (1993). *Protocol analysis: verbal reports as data*. Cambridge, MA: MIT Press.

Field, A. (2005). *Discovering statistics using SPSS*, 2nd ed. London: Sage Publications.

Field, A. (2005). *Discovering statistics: using SPSS*, 2nd ed. London: Thousand Oaks: Sage Publications.

Fisher, R. A. (1925; 1991). *Statistical methods, experimental design, and scientific inference*. Oxford: Oxford University Press.

Fox, S., Rainie, L., Larsen, E., Horrigan, J., Lenhart, A., Spooner, T. and Carter, C. (2001). Wired seniors. The Pew Internet and American Life Project. Retrieved 6 February 2008 from: http://www.pewinternet.org/pdfs/PIP_Wired_Seniors_Report.pdf/.

Fraenkel, J. R. and Wallen, N. E. (2006). *How to design and evaluate research in education*, 6th ed. Boston, MA: McGraw-Hill.

Friedman, T. L. (2006). *The world is flat: a brief history of the twenty-first century*. New York: Farrar, Straus and Giroux.

Furlong, M. S. (1989). An electronic community for older adults: the SeniorNet Network. *Journal of Communication*, 39 (3), 145–153.

Garton, L., Haythornthwaite, C. and Wellman, B. (1999). Studying on-line social networks. In S. Jones (Ed.), *Doing Internet research: critical issues and methods for examining the Net* (pp. 75–105). Thousand Oaks, CA: Sage Publications.

Gold, R. (1969). Roles in sociological field observation. In G. McCall and J. L. Simmons (Eds), *Issues in participant observation* (pp. 30–39). Reading, MA: Addison Wesley.

Goldhor, H. (1972). *An introduction to scientific research in librarianship*. Urbana, IL: University of Illinois.

Goldman, A. E. and MacDonald, S. S. (1987). *The group depth interview*. Englewood Cliffs, NJ: Prentice Hall.

Gordon, R. S. (2004). *The librarian's guide to writing for publication*. Lanham, the Scarecrow Press.

Gorman, M. (2003a). *The enduring library: technology tradition, and the quest for balance*. Chicago, IL: American Library Association.

Gorman, M. (2003b). Wither library education? Keynote speech at the Joint EUCLID/ALISE Conference, Postdam, Germany, 31 July.

Gorman, G. E. and Clayton, P. (2005). *Qualitative research for the information professional: a practical handbook*, 2nd ed. London: Facet Publishing.

Gray, D. (2004). *Doing research in the real world*. London: Sage Publications.

Griffiths, J. M. and King, D. W. (1986). *New directions in library and information science education*. Westport, CT: Greenwood Press Inc.

Grotzinger, L. (1981). Methodology of library science inquiry—past and present. In C. H. Busha (Ed.), *A library science research reader and bibliographic guide* (pp. 38–50). Littleton, CO: Libraries Unlimited.

Hara, N., Solomon, P., Kim, S-L. and Sonnenwald, D. H. (2003). An emerging view of scientific collaboration: scientists' perspectives on collaboration and factors that impact collaboration. *Journal of the American Society for Information Science and Technology*, 5 (10), 952–965.

Harbo, O. (1996). *Recent trends in library and information science education in Europe*. Paper presented at the 62nd

IFLA Council and General Conference, the Challenge of Change: Libraries and Economic Development, Beijing, 1996.

Hargens, L. L. (1988). Scholarly concensus and journal rejection rates. *American Sociological Review*, 53, 139–158.

Hart, C. (1998). *Doing a literature review: releasing the social science research imagination*. Thousand Oaks, CA: Sage Publications.

Haynes, E. B. (1996). Library-faculty partnerships in instruction. *Advances in Librarianship*, 20, 191–222.

Hernon, P. (1991). The elusive nature of research in LIS. In C. R. McClure and P. Hernon (Eds), *Library and information science research: perspectives and strategies for improvement* (pp. 3–10). Norwood, NJ: Ablex Publishing Corporation.

Hernon, P. (1994). *Statistics: a component of the research process*, (Rev.Ed.). Norwood, NJ: Ablex Publishing Corporation.

Hernon, P. (1994). Determination of sample size and selection of the sample: concepts, general sources and software. *College & Research Libraries*, 55, 171–179.

Hernon, P. (1999). Editorial: research in library and information science—reflections on the journal literature. *Journal of Academic Librarianship*, 25 (4), 263–266.

Hill, J. E. and Kerber, A. (1967). *Models, methods and analytical procedures in educational research*. Detroit, MI: Wayne State University Press.

Hook, S. (2005). Teaching librarians and writing center professionals in collaboration: complementary practices. In J. K. Elmborg and S. Hook (Eds), *Centers for learning: writing centers and libraries in collaboration* (pp. 21–41). Chicago, IL: Association of College and Research Libraries.

Houser, L. and Schrader, A. M. (1978). *The search for a scientific profession: library science education in the U.S. and Canada*. Metuchen, NJ: Scarecrow Press.

Hurt, C. D. (1992). The future of library science in higher education: a crossroads for library science and librarianship. *Advances in Librarianship*, 16, 153–181.

Iivonen, M. and Sonnenwald, D. H. (2000). The use of technology in international collaboration: two case studies. In N. Roderer, and D. Kraft (Eds), *Proceedings of the 63rd ASIS Annual Conference* (pp. 78–92). Medford, NJ: Information Today.

Jackson, S. L. (1963). Teaching of research in the library schools. *Library Journal*, 88, 2206–2207.

Jehl, J. and Kirst, M. W. (1993). Getting ready to provide school-linked services: what schools must do. *Education and Urban Society*, 25 (2), 153–165.

Johnson, W. B. and Mullen, C. A. (2007). *Write to the top: how to become a prolific academic*. New York: Pelgrave Macmillan.

Jorgensen, D. (1989). *Participant observation: a methodology for human studies*. London: Sage Publications.

Kagan, S. L. (1991). *United we stand: collaboration for child care and early education services*. New York: Teachers College Press.

Kajberg, L. and Leif Lorring, L. (2005). *European curriculum reflections on library and information science education*. Copenhagen: The Royal School of Library and Information Science.

Kerr, G. (2004). Shinkuro: tools for collaboration. Environmental Scans Blog. Available at: http://blog.real worldsystems.net/blog/_archives/2004/4/9/118359.html/.

Klobas, J. and Beesley, A. (2006). *Wikis: tools for information work and collaboration*. Oxford: Chandos.

Knievel, J. E., Wicht, H. and Silipigni, L. (2006). Use of circulation statistics and interlibrary loan data in collection management. *College & Research Libraries* 67 (1), 35–49.

Lancour, H. (1971). *The library school and research in librarianship in North America.* Paper presented at the meeting sponsored by the Committee on Library Education at the Council of the International Federation of Library Associations. 37th session, Liverpool, England, 2 September.

LeCompte, M., Preissle, J. and Tesch, R. (1993). *Ethnography and qualitative design in educational research*, 2nd ed. New York: Academic Press.

Leech, N. L., Barrett, K. C. and Morgan, G. A. (2005). *SPSS for intermediate statistics: use and interpretation*, 2nd ed. Mahwah, NJ: Lawrence Erlbaum. (Internet Resource).

Leedy, P. D. (1989). *Practical research: planning and design*, 4th ed. London: Collier Macmillan.

Lefever, S., Dal, M. and Matthiasdttir, A. (2007). Online data collection in academic research: advantages and limitations. *British Journal of Educational Psychology*, 38 (4), 574–582.

Lester, J. (1990). Education for Librarianship: a report card. *American Libraries*, 21 (6), 580–583.

Liao, Y., Finn, M. and Lu, J. (2007). Information seeking behavior of international graduate students versus American graduate students: a user study at Virginia Tech, 2005. *College & Research Libraries*, 68, 5–25.

Liebscher, P. (1998). Quantity with quality? Teaching quantitative and qualitative methods in an LIS Master's program. *Library Trends*, 46 (4), 669.

Litosseliti, L. (2003). *Using focus groups in research.* London: Continuum.

Lynch, B. P. (1998). The development of the academic library in American higher education and the role of the academic librarian. In T. F. Mech, and C. B. MacCabe (Eds),

Leadership and academic libraries (pp. 3–21). Westport, CT: Greenwood Press.

Lynch, B. P., Murray-Rust, C., Parker, S. E., Turner, D., Walker, D. P., Wilkinson, F. D. and Zimmerman, J. (2007). Attitudes of presidents and provosts on the University Library. *College & Research Libraries*, 68 (2), 213–227.

Lynch, M. J. (1984). Research and librarianship: an uneasy connection. *Library Trends*, 32, 361–383.

Lynch, B. P. (2008). Library education: its past, its present, its future. *Library Trends*, 56 (4), 931–953.

Manski, C. F. and Molinari, F. (2008). Skip sequencing: a decision problem in questionnaire design. *Annals of Applied Statistics*, 2 (1), 264–285.

Marcum, D. B. (1997). Transforming the curriculum; transforming the profession. *American Libraries*, 27 (1), 35–38.

Martin, L. (1957). Research in education for librarianship. *Research in Librarianship*, 6 (October): 207.

Marshall, J. G. (1989). *An introduction to research methods for health sciences librarians.* Courses for continuing education. Chicago, IL: Medical Library Association.

Mattessich, P. and Monsey, B. (1992). *Collaboration: what makes it work.* St Paul, MN: Amherst H. Wilder Foundation.

Mellon, C. A. (1986). Library anxiety: a grounded theory and its development. *College & Research Libraries*, 47 (March), 160.

Merriam-Webster Inc. (2001). *Merriam-Webster's collegiate dictionary*, 10th ed. Springfield, MA: Merriam-Webster.

Morgan, J. A. (2004). *SPSS for introductory statistics: use and interpretation.* Mahwah, NJ: Lawrence Erlbaum. (Internet Resource).

Morris, A. (2002). *From idea to impact: a guide to the research process.* London: Department of Education and Skills.

Nasri, W. Z. (1972). Education in library and information science. In A. Kent and H. Lancour (Eds), *Encyclopedia of library and information science*, Vol. 7 (pp. 416–465). New York: Marcel Dekker.

National Opinion Research Center. http://www.norc.org/channels/.

Nie, N., Hillygus, S. and Erbing, L. (2002). Internet use, interpersonal relations and sociability: findings from a detailed time diary study. In B. Wellman (Ed.), *The Internet in everyday life* (pp. 215–243). London: Blackwell Publishers.

Norlin, E. and Winters, C. M. (2002). *Usability testing for library Web sites: a hand-on guide*. Chicago, IL: American Library Association.

Palfrey, J. and Gasser, U. (2008). *Born digital: understanding the first generation of digital natives*. New York: Basic books.

Pallant, J. (2007). *Survival manual: a step by step guide to data analysis using SPSS*, 3rd ed. Maidenhead: Open University Press.

Paris, M. (1988). *Library school closings: four case studies*. Metuchen, NJ: The Scarecrow Press, Inc.

Paris, M. (1990). Why library schools fail. *Library Journal*, 115 (16), 38–42.

Parker, G. M. (2008). *Team players and teamwork: new strategies for developing collaboration*. 2nd ed. San Francisco, CA: Jossey Bass.

Patton, M. Q. (2001). *Qualitative research and evaluation methods*, 3rd ed. Newbury Park, CA: Sage Publications.

Pendlebury, D. A. (1991). Science, citation and funding. *Science*, 251, 1410–1411.

Pensky, M. (2001). Digital natives, digital immigrants. *On the Horizon*, 9 (5), 1–6.

Pitkin, R. M. and Branagan, M. A. (1998). Can the accuracy of abstracts be improved by providing specific instructions? A randomized controlled trial. *JAMA*, 280, 67–269.

Powell, R. R. and Connaway, L. S. (2004). *Basic research methods for librarians*, 4th ed. Westport, CT: Libraries Unlimited.

Public Libraries in the United States: Their history, condition and management. (1876). Washington DC: US Bureau of Education.

Raspa, D. and Ward, D. (2000). *The collaborative imperative: librarians and faculty working together in the information universe.* Chicago, IL: Association of College and Research Libraries.

ur Rehman, S., Al-Ansari, H. and Yousef, N. (2002). Coverage of competencies in the curriculum of information studies: an international perspective. *Education for Information*, 20 (3/4), 199–215.

Richardson, J. (1982). *The spirit of inquiry: the Graduate Library School at Chicago*, 1C921–51. Chicago, IL: American Library Association.

Robbins-Carter, J. and Seavey, C. A. (1986). The master's degree: basic preparation for professional practice. *Library Trends*, 34, 561–590.

Rudenstam, K. E. and Newton, R. R. (2007). *Surviving your dissertation: a comprehensive guide to content and process.* 3rd ed. Thousand Oaks, CA: Sage Publications Inc.

Rullman, F. (1874). Die bibliothekesinrichtungskende zum Thiele einer geineinssamen organization die fen. Freinberg. In *Public libraries in the United States: their history, condition and management.* (1876). Washington DC: US Bureau of Education, p. xxiii.

Saiful, A. (nd) *The comparative study of LIS education in India, UK and USA.* Retrieved 6 May 2007 from http://drtc.isibang.ac.in/~saiful/colloq/lis_edu.html/.

Salkind, N. J. (2009). *Exploring research*, 7th ed. Upper Saddle River, NJ: Pearson Prentice Hall.

Schrage, M. (1990). *Shared minds: the new technologies of collaboration*. New York: Random House.

Schrettinger, M. W. (1834). Handbuch der bibliothek-wissenschaft, besonders zum ge brauche der michi-bibliothekare, welche ihre privatbuchersammlungen selbst einrichten wollen. Auch als leit-faden zu vorlesunger uber die bibliothek-wissenschaft zu bebrauchen. Wien: F. Beck. In *Public Libraries in the United States of America: their history, condition and management* (1876), p. xxv.

Seaman, S. (2007). Estimating salary compression in an ARL institution: a University of Colorado at Boulder case study. *College & Research Libraries*, 68 (5), 388–404.

Shaughnessy, T. W. (1976). Research in the 70's: problems and prospects. *California Librarian*, 37, 44–52.

Shera, J. H. (1964). Darwin, Bacon and research in librarianship. *Library Trends*, 13, 144.

Shera, J. H. (1972). *Foundations of education for librarianship*. New York: Becker and Hayes, p. 419.

Siegel, P. (1971). Prestige in the American occupational structure. Ph.D. Dissertation, University of Chicago.

Siegel, S. and Castellan, N. J. (1988). *Nonparametric statistics for the behavioral sciences*, 2nd ed. New York: McGraw-Hill.

Silvia, P. J. (2007). *How to write a lot: a practical guide to productive academic writing*. Washington, DC: American Psychological Association.

Stoffle, C. J. and Leeder, K. (2005). Practitioners and library education: a crisis of understanding. *Journal of Education for Library and Information Science*, 46 (4), 313–320.

Swisher, R. and McClure, C. R. (1984). *Research for decision making: methods for librarians*. Chicago, IL: American Library Association.

Tautman, R. (1954). *A history of the School of Library Service, Columbia University*. New York: Columbia University Press, p. vii.

Taylor, H. (2000). Does Internet research work? Comparing electronic survey results with telephone survey. *International Journal of Market Research*, 42 (1), 51–63.

Van den Haak, M. J., de Jong, M. D. T. and Schellens, P. J. (2004). Employing Think-Aloud protocols and constructive interaction to test the usability of online library catalogues: a methodological comparison. *Interacting with Computers*, 16 (6), 1153–1170.

Vaughn, J. (1976). Occupational categories and occupational prestige scales. In N. Lin (Ed.), *Foundations of social research* (pp. 415–428). New York: McGraw-Hill.

Walliman, N. (2005). *Your research project: a step-by-step guide for the first-time researcher.* London: Sage Publications.

Walter, S. and Eodice, M. (2007). Meeting the student learning imperative: supporting and sustaining collaboration between academic libraries and student services programs. *Research Strategies*, 20, 219–225.

Ward, J. and Hiller, S. (2005). Usability testing interface design, and portals. *Journal of Library Administration*, 43 (1/2), 155–171.

Wasserman, P. (1972). *The new librarianship: a challenge for change.* New York: Bowker, p. 135.

Welch, M. (2000). Collaboration as a tool for inclusion, In S. E. Wade (Ed.), *Inclusive education: a casebook and readings for prospective and practicing teachers* (pp. 71–96). Mahwah, NJ: Erlbaum Associates.

White, H. (1983). Accreditation and the pursuit of excellence. *Journal of Education for Librarianship*, 23 (4), 253–263.

White, H. S. and Paris, M. (1985). Employer preferences and the library education curriculum. *Library Quarterly*, 55, 1–33.

Whitmire, E. (2001). The relationship between undergraduate's background characteristics and college experiences, and their academic library use. *College & Research Libraries*, 62, 528–540.

Wiegand, W. (2002). This month 149 years ago. *American Libraries*, 33 (June/July), 122.

Williamson, C. C. (1923). *Training for library service; a report prepared for the Carnegie Corporation of New York*. New York: Carnegie Corporation.

Williamson, C. (1931). The place of research in Library Science. *Library Quarterly*, 1, 3.

Wilson, H. W. (2008). Library Literature & Information Science full text: a unique working tool created by librarians for librarians. Available at: http://www .hwwilson.com/databases/liblit.htm/.

Wilson, A. M. and Hemanson, R. (1998). Educating and training library practitioners: a comparative history with trends and recommendations. *Library Trends*, 46 (3), 467–504.

Wright, K. B. (2000a). Computer-mediated social support, older adults, and coping. *Journal of Communication*, 50 (30), 100–118.

Wright, K. B. (2000b). The communication of social support within an on-line community for older adults: a qualitative analysis of the SeniorNet community. *Qualitative Research Reports in Communication*, 1 (2), 33–43.

Wynar, L. R. (1970). Phase of statistics in the library science curriculum. *Journal of Education for Librarianship*, 11 (Fall 1970), 155–162.

Young, V. L. (1993). Focus on focus groups. *College & Research Libraries News*, 7, 391.

Yun, G. W. and Trumbo, C. W. (2000). Comparative response to a survey executed by post, email, and web form, *Journal of Computer-Mediated Communication*, 6 (1). Retrieved 6 February 2008 from: http://jcmc.indiana .edu/vo16/issue1/yun.html/.

Zuckerman, H. and Merton, R. K. (1971). Patterns of evaluation in science: institutionalization, structure and functions of the referee system. *Minerva*, 9, 66–100.

Additional reading

Afzal, W. (2006). An argument for the increased use of qualitative research in LIS. *Emporia State Research Studies*, 43 (1), 22–25.

Alexander, J., Giesen, B., Munch, R. and Smelser, N. (Eds) (1987). *The micro-macro link*. Berkeley: University of California Press.

American Library Association (1975). Statement on professional ethics. *American Libraries*, (April), 231.

Armstrong, A., Branley, S. and Lewis, K. M. (2006). Usability testing for of a customizable library Web portal. *College & Research Libraries*, 67 (2), 146–163.

Bekker, J. (1976). *Professional ethics and its application to librarianship*. Ph.D. Dissertation, Case Western Reserve University.

Bell, J. (2005). *Doing your research project; a guide for first-time researchers in education, health and social science*, 4th ed. Maidenhead, Berkshire: Open University Press.

Bolduc, A. P. (2008). Surveying user needs in an international context: a qualitative case study from the ILO, Geneva. *The International Information & Library Review*, 40, 1–9.

Bradford, J. T., Kannon, K. E. and Ryan, S. M. (1996). Designing and implementing a faculty Internet workshop: a collaborative effort of academic computing services and university library. *Research Strategies*, 14, 234–245.

Bradley, J. and Sutton, B. (1993). Reframing the paradigm debate. *Library Quarterly*, 63 (4), 405–410.

Burke, J. and Christensen, L. (2000). *Educational research: quantitative and qualitative approaches*. Boston, MA: Allyn and Bacon.

Cohen, C. (1995). Faculty liaison: a cooperative venture in bibliographic instruction. *Reference Librarian*, 51/52, 161–169.

Cook, D. (2000). Creating connections: a review of the literature. In D. Raspa, and D. Ward (Eds), *The collaborative imperative: librarians and faculty working together in the information universe*. Chicago, IL: American Library Association.

Chou, J-R. and Hsiao, S-W. (2007). A usability study on human-computer interface for middle-aged learners. *Computers in Human Behavior*, 23 (4), 2040–2063.

Davis, D. G. Jr. and Jucker, J. M. (1989). *American library history: a comprehensive guide to the literature*. Santa Barbara, CA: ABC-Clio.

DeWitt, D. (Ed.) (2001). *Evaluating the twenty-first century library: the Association of Research Libraries new measures initiative, 1997–2001*. New York: The Haworth Press Inc.

Dimitroff, A. (1992). Research in health sciences library and information science. *Library & Information Science Research*, 80, 251–262.

Dimitroff, A. (1995). Research for special libraries: a quantitative analysis of the literature. *Special Libraries*, 86, 256–264.

Doll, C. A. (2005). *Collaboration and the school library media specialist*. Lanham, MD: Scare Crow Press Inc.

Gerstein, C. W. (1995). Liaison with teaching faculty: effective strategies for collaborative collection development. *Public & Access Services Quarterly*, 1 (4), 85–90.

Glazier, J. D. and Powell, R. R. (Eds) (1992). *Qualitative research in information management*. Englewood, CO: Libraries Unlimited.

Gorman, M. (1990). A bogus and dismal science or the eggplant that ate library schools. *American Libraries*, 21, 462–463.

Harvey, C. A. (2008). Collaboration connections. *School Library Media Activities Monthly*, 24 (9), 20–22.

Himmelman, A. T. (1996). On the theory and practice of transformational collaboration: from social service to social justice. In C. Huxham (Ed.), *Creating collaborative advantage* (pp. 19–43). London: Sage.

Hinchliffe, J. (2000). Faculty directed library use instruction: a single class retrospective study. *Research Strategies*, 17, 281–289.

Hinchliffe, L. J. and Woodard, B. S. (2001). Instruction. In R. E. Bopp and L. E. Smith (Eds), *Reference and information services* (3rd ed.) (pp. 177–209). Englewood, CO: Libraries Unlimited.

Horn, J. (1998). Qualitative research literature: a bibliographic essay—qualitative research. *Library Trends*, 46 (4), 602–615.

Jackson, S. L., Herling, E. and Josey, E. J. (Eds) (1976). *A century of service: librarianship in the United States of America and Canada*. Chicago, IL: American Library Association.

Jones, D. Y. (2007). How much do the 'best' colleges spend on libraries? Using college rankings to provide library financial benchmarks. *College & Research Libraries*, 68 (4), 343–351.

Jones, S. (Ed.). (1999). *Doing Internet research: critical issues and methods for examining the Net*. Newbury Park, CA: Sage Publications.

Julien, H. (1996). A content analysis of the recent information needs and uses literature. *Library and Information Science Research*, 18, 53–65.

Kaplan, B. and Maxwell, J. A. (1994). *Qualitative research methods for evaluating computer information systems*. In

J. G. Anderson, C. E. Avdin and S. J. Jay (Eds), *Evaluating health care information systems: methods and applications* (pp. 45–68). Thousand Oaks, CA: Sage Publications.

Knievel, J. E. (2008). Instruction to faculty and graduate students: a tutorial to teach publication strategies. *portal: Libraries and the Academy*, 8 (2), 175–186.

Krosnick, J. (1999). Survey research. *Annual Review of Psychology*, 50, 537–567.

Kussrow, P. G. and Laurence, H. (1993). Instruction in developing grant proposals: a librarian–faculty partnership. *Research Strategies*, 11, 47–51.

Lalleman, R. and Wesseling, M. (2008). Knowledge sharing through collaboration in development studies: The Focuss.Info Initiative. *Information Development*, 24, 151–155.

Letnikova, G. (2003). Usability testing of academic library Web sites: a selective annotated bibliography. *Internet Reference Services Quarterly* 8 (4), 53–68.

Lincoln, Y. (2002). Insights into library services and users from qualitative research. *Library and Information Science Research*, 24, 3–16.

Lincoln, Y. S. and Guba, E. G. (1985). *Naturalistic inquiry.* Newbury Park, CA: Sage Publications.

McClure, C. R. and Hert, C. A. (1991). *Specialization in library/information science education: issues, scenarios and the need for action.* Paper presented at the Conference on specialization in Library/Information Science Education, Ann Arbor, Michigan, 6–8 November 1991.

Mann, C. and Stewart, F. (2002). Internet interviewing. In J. F. Gubrium and J. A. Holstein (Eds), *Handbook of interview research* (pp. 603–628). Thousand Oaks, CA: Sage Publications.

Markey, K. (2004). Current educational trends in the Information and Library Science curriculum. *Journal of Education for Library and Information Science*, 45, 317–339.

Mason, R. O., McKenney, J. L. and Copeland, D. G. (1997). An historical method for MIS research: steps and assumptions. *MIS Quarterly*, September, 307–319.

Merriam, S. B. (1988). *The case study research in education*. San Francisco, CA: Jossey-Bass.

Metoyer-Duran, C. and Hernon, P. (1994). Problem statements in research proposals and published research: a case study of researchers' viewpoints. *Library and Information Science Research*, 16, 105–118.

Miller, M. (1996). What to expect from library school graduates. *Information Technology and Libraries*, 15 (10), 45–47.

Miles, M. B. and Huberman, A. M. (1994). *Qualitative data analysis: an expanded source book*, 2nd ed. Thousand Oaks, CA: Sage.

Minichiello, V. (1990). *In-depth interviewing: researching people*. Melbourne: Cheshire.

Mouly, G. J. (1970). *The science of education research*, 2nd Ed. New York: Van Nostrand Reinhold.

Mudrock, T. (2002). Revising ready reference sites: listening to users through server statistics and query logs. *Reference and User Services Quarterly*, 42, 321–343.

Mulder, U. (1992). Building bridges across an academic community. *Australian Academic & Research Libraries*, 23, 175–178.

Myers, M. D. and Avison, D. E. (Eds). (2002). *Qualitative research in information systems: a reader*. London: Sage Publications.

Nichols, J. W. (2001). Sharing a vision: information literacy partnerships K-16. Librarians at Wayne State University offer workshops for local high school students. *College & Research Libraries News*, 62 (3), 275–7, 285.

Ochola, J. N. (2002). Use of circulation statistics and interlibrary loan data in collection management. *Collection Management*, 27, 1–13.

Ragin, C. and Becker, H. (Eds). (1992). *What is a case?* New York: Cambridge University Press.

Reece, E. J. (1936). *Curriculum in library schools*. New York: Columbia University Press.

Reed, S. R. (1971). The curriculum of library schools today: a historical overview. In H. Goldhor (Ed.). *Education for librarianship: the design of the curriculum of library schools* (pp. 19–45). Urbana, Champaign, IL: Graduate School of Library Science, University of Illinois.

Rothstein, S. (1966). The ideal faculty member: qualifications and experience. *Journal of Education for Librarianship*, 16, 173–182.

Scott, R. W. (1965). Field methods in the study of organizations. In J. G. March (Ed.). *Handbook of organizations* (pp. 261–304). Chicago, IL: Rand McNally.

Shores, I. (1972). *Library education*. Littleton, CO: Libraries Unlimited.

Stake, R. E. (1994). Case studies. In N. K. Denzin and Y. S. Lincoln (Eds), *Handbook of qualitative research* (pp. 236–246). Thousand Oaks, CA: Sage.

Suter, V., Alexander, B. and Kaplan, P. (2005). The future of FTF. EDUCAUSE Review, 40 (1). Available at: http://www.educause.edu/apps/er/erm0514.asp?bhcp=0511/.

Van, S. K. (1961). *Training for librarianship before 1923*. Chicago, IL: American Library Association.

Vickery, R. C. (1975). Academic research in library and information studies. *Journal of Librarianship*, 7, 153–60.

Werner, O. and Schoeptfle, G. M. (1987). *Systematic fieldwork*: Vol. 1, *Foundations if ethnography and interviewing*. Newbury Park, CA: Sage.

Williamson, C. C. (1919). Some present day aspects of library training. *ALA Bulletin*, 13, 120.

Williamson, W. L. (1986). A century of students. *Library Trends*, 34 930, 433–449.

Wright, K. B. (2005). Researching Internet-based populations: advantages and disadvantages of online survey research, online questionnaire authoring software packages, and Web survey services. *Journal of Computer-Mediated Communications*, 10 (3), article 11. Retrieved 6 February 2008 from: http://jcmc.indiana.edu/vol10/issue3/wright.html/.

Wrubel, L. and Schmidt, K. (2007). Usability testing of a metasearch interface: a case study. *College & Research Libraries*, 68 (4), 292–311.

Ye, Y. (2008). The outreach symposium: a model of library collaboration. *College & Research Libraries News*, 69 (7). Retrieved on 7 November 2008 from: http://www.acrl.org/ala/mgrps/divs/acrl/publications/crlnews/2008/jul/july.cfm/.

Yin, R. K. (1989). *Case study research: design and methods*, 2nd ed. Newbury Park, CA: Sage.

Young, J. (1995). Faculty collaboration and academic librarians. *Catholic Library World,* 66, 17.

Zvacek, S. M. and Walter, S. (2005). *High velocity change: creating collaborative learning environments (ECAR Research Bulletin*, 2005, no. 15). Boulder, CO: EDUCAUSE Center for Applied Research.

Glossary

Analysis of variance (ANOVA): a statistical procedure that tests whether group means differ.

Bivariate correlation: a correlation between two variables.

Chi-square test: a non-parametric test of statistical significance appropriate when the data are in the form of frequency counts; it compares frequencies actually observed in a study with expected frequencies to see whether they are significantly different.

Coefficient of determination: the proportion of variance in one variable explained by a second variable.

Contingency table: a table representing cross-tabulation of two or more categorical variables.

Dependent variable: another term for outcome variable.

Heteroscedasticity: this occurs when at each point on the predictor variable, the spread of residuals, is different. In other words the residuals at each level of the predictor variable have unequal variances.

Histogram: frequency distribution.

Homoscedasticity: an assumption in regression analysis that the residuals at cach point of the predictor variable have equal variances.

Hypothesis: a prediction of what the results of the study would be.

Kurtosis: measures the degree to which scores cluster in the tails of frequency distribution.

Logistic regression: is a part of a category of statistical models called a generalized linear model.

Multiple regression: the outcome is predicted by linear combination of two or more predictor variables.

Nominal data: numbers just represent names.

Non-parametric tests: a set of statistical tests that do not rely on the assumptions of the parametric tests.

Normal distribution: probability distribution of a variable. It is perfectly symmetrical, no skew, no kurtosis.

ODBC (Open Database Connectivity): a standard database access method developed by the SQL Access Group in 1992. The goal of ODBC is to make it possible to access any data from any application regardless of which database management system is handling the data.

Pearson's correlation coefficient: standardized measure of the strength of the relationship between two variables. The value could be anywhere from −1, which means as one variable changes, the other changes in the opposite direction by the same amount, through zero (no change in any of the variables) to +1, which means as one variable changes, the other changes in the same direction by the same amount.

Predictor variable: a variable that is used to predict value of another variable called the outcome variable.

Reliability: ability of a measure to produce consistent results when the same entities are subjected to the same conditions.

Residual: the difference between the value a model predicts and the observed value in the data.

Skew: measure of the symmetry of a frequency distribution.

SQL (Structured Query Language): standard language for accessing and manipulating databases. It is designed for the retrieval and management of data in relational databases.

Standard deviation (SD): the most stable measure of variability.

Syntax: pre-defined written commands that instruct a software program, e.g. SPSS, what is to be done.

Index